The Emergence of Liberty in the Modern World

The Emergence of Liberty in the Modern World

The Influence of Calvin on Five Governments from the 16th Through 18th Centuries

Douglas F. Kelly

P&R
PUBLISHING
P.O. BOX 817 • PHILLIPSBURG • NEW JERSEY 08865-0817

Manufactured in the United States of America

Library of Congress Cataloging-in-Publication Data

Kelly, Douglas, 1943–
The emergence of liberty in the modern world : the influence of Calvin on five governments from the 16th through the 18th centuries : Calvin's Geneva, Huguenot France, Knox's Scotland, Puritan England, Colonial America / Douglas F. Kelly.
p. cm.
Includes bibliographical references and index.
ISBN-10: 0-87552-297-1
ISBN-13: 978-087552-297-5
1. Church and state—Reformed Church—History. 2. Church and state—Presbyterian Church—History. 3. Church and state—Europe—History. 4. Church and state—United States—History. 5. Reformed Church—Doctrines—History. 6. Presbyterian Church—Doctrines—History. 7. Calvinism—History. 8. Calvin, Jean, 1509–1564—Influence. 9. Calvin, Jean, 1509–1564—Contributions in doctrine of church and state. I. Title.
BV630.2.K45 1992
322'.1'09—dc20 92-19308

To

MARTHA McCRUMMEN FRASER KELLY,

my daughter,
with love and appreciation

Tell out, my soul, the greatness of His might!
Powers and dominions lay their glory by;
Proud hearts and stubborn wills are put to flight,
The hungry fed, the humble lifted high.

Tell out, my soul, the glories of His Word!
Firm is His promise, and His mercy sure.
Tell out, my soul, the greatness of the Lord
To children's children and for evermore!

(From the hymn-paraphrase of the Virgin Mary's *Magnificat*,
adapted from *The New English Bible*, by
the Rev. Timothy Dudley-Smith, Bishop of Norwich.)

Contents

Preface

THIS BOOK was originally inspired by my participation in the Jurisprudence Panel of the Christian Legal Society, which began meeting in the early 1980s. Legal scholars and theologians of the major Christian traditions that have been influential in American history (such as Anglican, Baptist, Lutheran, Mennonite, Reformed, and Roman Catholic) met together from time to time for several years. Our basic task was to attempt to understand what our respective Christian traditions had historically understood and practiced concerning law, authority, liberty, and responsibility, and especially their norms for church-state relations. There was also some thought that as we shared these denominational particularities together as a panel, we might be able to forge some general guidelines for Christian lawyers, judges, and others, who wished to discern what is just in contemporary struggles affecting religious liberty.

In the end of our sessions, our panel was unable to complete its ambitious program. But I think all who participated were greatly stimulated by one another "as iron sharpens iron" in their research on the questions of form and freedom in relation to the missions of church and state. While we did not secure the funding to finish the task of publishing a volume on each tradition, several members of the panel (or experts chosen by them) have since that time indeed been stimulated to issue monographs giving guidance on controversial matters touching law and liberty in their own tradition. Such material is now becoming available and will, we trust, make a contribution to religious liberty in years ahead. This particular volume, which deals with the integral role of Calvinism in the emergence of liberty from the sixteenth to the eighteenth centuries, is part of the literature spurred by those earlier efforts. It is hoped that this book and other material like it may in some way help fulfill the original vision by providing clearly researched material from the past to give light to those who are facing issues of civil and religious liberty in the present and future.

Although the Jurisprudence Panel was no longer meeting by the time I wrote this volume, so that their counsel was not available to me, I was greatly helped by Curran Tiffany, who had guided the earlier work of the panel. After a notable legal career, Mr. Tiffany has worked with both the Christian Legal Society and the National Association of Evangelicals, particularly on matters relating to religious liberty and the intersecting roles of church and state. He willingly gave of his time to go over the entire manuscript and offered many helpful criticisms and suggestions, which have, I believe, considerably strengthened the final product. Any mistakes or other weaknesses that remain, however, are mine and not his.

I wrote this volume during a sabbatical leave in 1988, which was kindly granted to me by the Administration and Executive Committee of Reformed Theological Seminary, Jackson, Mississippi, where I teach. Many friends helped in various ways to make it possible for us to spend this study leave in Scotland. The Young Seekers Sunday School Class of First Presbyterian Church in Jackson, led at that time by Dean Fulghom, assisted us, as did Arthur Stringer, Charles Williams, Bo Bowen, George Whitten, and several others, including an anonymous black Baptist church in Jackson. Friends in Dillon, South Carolina, helped make our preparations to leave easier. Some of them are Phil Brown, Harry Gibbons, Jim Atkins, John E. Hobeika, William Hobeika, and Bruce Price. I also record with gratitude the kind assistance of Florence Baptist Temple in Florence, South Carolina, whose pastor is Dr. William T. Monroe. Friends in both the First Presbyterian Church and Second Presbyterian Church of Yazoo City, Mississippi, stood with us, as did the Rev. William

Fulton, pastor of the United Methodist Church in Thorndale, Texas.

In Edinburgh we were blessed to stay in pleasant accommodations through the good offices of Rev. Dr. Frank Gibson and to work at Rutherford House, then directed by Dr. Nigel Cameron. Miss Janella Glover, administrative secretary at Rutherford House, was of constant help to me in my work. Ros Mills of Melbourne, Australia, (now Mrs. Christopher Thorne) served as our children's nanny during our sabbatical and afterward. The Rev. William Still of Aberdeen and Miss V. G. S. Cornish-Browne of the same city encouraged us in many ways during our stay in Scotland.

My thinking on the connections between Calvinist theology and experience and the rise of modern liberty was enriched and stimulated more than I can say by personal discussions with many British and American scholars in various related fields of study. Professor Francis Lyall of the Faculty of Law in Aberdeen University gave me many insights and fruitful bibliography, as did Dr. William Storrar, then a Church of Scotland minister in Carluke (and author of *Scottish Identity: A Christian Vision*), now of the University of Edinburgh. We met several times with great profit to me. Professor of American History, Mark Noll, of Wheaton College sharpened my thinking in areas related to the American constitutional experience. Christian writer and modern-day reformer Jean-Marc Berthoud of Lausanne shared insights on the historic Christian background of Western liberty. Several discussions with Professors Thomas F. Torrance and Ronald S. Wallace in Edinburgh shed light in more than one area of this field of study. Professor Torrance also kindly read through and critiqued the complete manuscript. Dean Courthial (now retired from the Faculty of Theology at Aix-en-Provence) read over the manuscript and particularly gave helpful criticisms of the chapter on the French Huguenots. Lord MacKay of Clashfearn, Lord High Chancellor of the United Kingdom, generously gave of his time to read through the third and fourth chapters in this volume.

Of course, I make no claim of having the approval of these scholars for the views offered in this book. I cannot fail to thank them for their help, but would not wish to charge them with any of the mistakes or peculiarities of this volume. The final responsibility for this work, for whatever it is worth, must rest at my door. And at our very best, in the words of St. Paul, ". . . we know in part . . ." (I Cor. 13:9).

The Rev. Steve Froelich of Reformed Theological Seminary entered the text of this book into the computer. Dr. Luder Whitlock, President of Reformed Theological Seminary, and Mr. Lyn Perez, Vice President of Reformed Theological Seminary in Orlando, Florida, have encouraged me through this entire process. Thom Notaro of Presbyterian and Reformed Publishing Company has given sound guidance through the final editorial stage. My student assistant, Russ Ragon, has been of great help in correcting page proofs. From first to last, I thank all of these talented friends from the bottom of my heart.

Introduction

THIS VOLUME traces the development of Calvinist thought on church-state relations and related subjects from the sixteenth through the eighteenth centuries in five different governments (four countries and one city-state). First, we study the emergence and development of the thought of John Calvin in the context of the Genevan city-state during the mid-sixteenth century. Second, we trace the radicalization, systematization, and slight secularization of Calvin's thoughts on civil resistance and constitutional rights among his French Huguenot followers during the 1570s. In the third chapter, we survey the development of aspects of Calvin's thought relating to covenant concepts of church and state in Scotland from the mid-sixteenth century through the eighteenth. Chapter 4 charts the struggles and results of the Calvinist Puritan experiment, which was part of the English revolution of the seventeenth century. The final chapter traces the influence of these varied national Calvinist experiences on the American colonies leading up to the War of Independence and constitutional settlement in the late eighteenth century.

In this volume we do not study the Netherlands, another country heavily influenced by Calvinism, largely because, through the eighteenth century the Dutch historical experience and church-state theory was not substantially different from the French Huguenot and

Scottish. In the nineteenth century however the work of the great Dutch Calvinist scholars William Groen Van Prinsterer and Abraham Kuyper represented the greatest development in Calvinist thought on law, authority, and church-state questions since the time of Calvin, Knox, and the French Huguenot tractarians. But since this study restricts itself to the sixteenth through the eighteenth centuries, the remarkable developments of nineteenth-century Dutch Calvinist thought must be reserved for another volume.

1

John Calvin and Geneva

A RECENT BIOGRAPHER of John Calvin has noted that secular historians, with their great interest in the pivotal significance of the sixteenth century for the modern world of capitalism, science, revolution, democracy, secularism, and empiricism, have generally neglected the seminal importance of Calvin in that time of massive transition.[1] The significance of Calvin's work is probably even less apparent in the contemporary disciplines of law and political science. The generally secular intellectual environment of our times sees religious concerns as peripheral to the central questions of law and authority, economics, and politics. That makes it difficult for us to transport ourselves back into the pre-Enlightenment atmosphere of Renaissance and Reformation Europe, when relationships between God and man or church and state were crucial to interpreting and shaping profound changes in the economic, cultural, and political spheres of life.

It is of course necessary to penetrate this earlier world of sixteenth-century thought and action if we are to understand our own political institutions—their origins and their foundational assumptions concerning law and right, order and authority, tolerance and freedom, or individualism and collectivism. The thought and work of John Calvin form one of the most powerful responses to the great European upheaval generally known as the Protestant Reformation.

Calvin's work not only constituted a *response* to revolutionary forces that were abroad when he came into prominence as a religious leader; it also *contributed* greatly to that European upheaval. His theology, the institutions that it engendered, and the questions it raised have played a major part in shaping all of the post-Reformation world.

Calvin and the Calvinist legacy continue to bear an influence—perhaps the stronger and deeper for the very fact that its roots are largely unperceived—on nearly all the major issues that have both guided and periodically agitated Western nations. For example, concerning the proper ordering of society such issues would include: religious and civil liberties; the interrelations, stability, and change of ecclesiastical and civil structures; and the issues of ultimate authority, or of right and wrong. Repeated attempts to deal with these questions, so important to Calvin and his successors, have taken varying forms over the generations. The approach of Calvin himself, and then the developments among his French Huguenot successors and the still different Scottish Reformers, English and New English Puritans, and at length American colonial patriots, demonstrate definite continuities, strong differences, and above all, historical adaptations to the shifting realities of the cultures in which the theological-intellectual heritage was being lived out. These related but varying approaches stemming from John Calvin must be considered part of the vital sinews, which—for all their hiddenness—have helped to hold together a skeletal system of political, economic, and religious life in the Western nation states for the last four hundred years.

Calvin's Lifelong Political Concern

John Calvin was born in Noyon, Northern France, in 1509 and died in Geneva in 1564. Although primarily a scholar, theologian, and preacher, as well as ecclesiastical statesman, he showed a strong political concern throughout his entire life. This political interest was evident even before his conversion (which seems to have occurred about 1533-34),[2] as we may note in his 1532 *Commentary on Seneca's De Clementia*. That commentary is in many respects an example of the sixteenth-century humanist genre of "a mirror for princes," which is concerned with equity for the people. Calvin's concern for a good form of government increased over the next four years, a time during which he was converted. He went on to produce his first edition of *The Institutes of the Christian Religion* in 1536. Ford Lewis Battles has suggested that the first edition of *The Institutes* can be understood as a sort of political treatise.[3] Its overriding concern with proper government is shown in the opening epistle, in which Calvin dedicated *The Institutes* to King Francis I of France (in effect, an apology for the persecuted evangelicals in France). This same governmental concern is dealt with again in considerable detail in the last chapter, "On Freedom, and Ecclesiastical and Civil Power."

In the middle and later years of his life, Calvin would write many letters to leading political figures in various parts of Europe, as well as regularly commenting on the shifting political situation in letters to his personal friends. He dedicated various commentaries to rulers as an encouragement to continue the work of Reformation in their countries. The commentaries on the Canonical Epistles honored Edward VI of England; the commentary on Isaiah was dedicated to Elizabeth I; and those on Hebrews to Sigismund, king of Poland.

Calvin's interest in statecraft went well beyond the ecclesiastical ramifications. After he had drafted the *Ecclesiastical Ordinances* for Geneva in 1541, the satisfied town councils asked him to take time off from his preaching ministry in order to codify the purely civil and constitutional laws of Geneva.[4] Calvin was well able to handle the complex details and overarching principles of legal codification because of his earlier training as a lawyer under some of the most famous legal scholars of his day. His Renaissance education, which combined both theological-philosophical and legal scholarship, goes far toward explaining the lifelong and fruitful marriage in his thought and activity between theological and legal concerns.

Medieval and Renaissance Influences

In 1523, at age fourteen, Calvin began his higher education in Paris, first at the College de la Marche, where he had the great advantage of tutoring in Latin by the renowned Mathurin Cordier.

Soon Calvin transferred to that stronghold of conservative orthodoxy, the College de Montaigu, which was frequented by such sixteenth-century notables as Erasmus, Ignatius Loyola, and Rabelais. Of great theological (and indeed, legal) influence on young Calvin here was the Scots Scotist, conciliar theologian and historian, John Major (or Mair), one of the last and greatest of the late medieval scholastic scholars. The initiation Major gave Calvin into the medieval and patristic Catholic heritage, his explication of more recent conciliar themes, his realist epistemology, and his own intensely practical approach to theology gave to Calvin's fertile and powerful mind a lasting orientation, which—for all his rejection of "papistry" and "the schoolmen"—profoundly shaped his thought and actions to the last.[5]

For centuries Protestant historiography has tended to neglect the influence of late medieval Catholicism upon the Reformers, but in recent decades this lacuna is being filled in by such scholars as F. Wendel,[6] H. Oberman,[7] T. F. Torrance,[8] and R. Kingdon.[9] The renewal of interest in the Reformers' late medieval Catholic heritage aids us in tracing very important continuities (and discontinuities) between Calvin and the Western Catholic tradition. These are particularly apposite to an understanding of Calvin's continually interrelating theology and law. Calvin's teacher, Major, like his more famous student, also combined an avid interest in civil questions and constitutional history, with an erudite commitment to ancient Catholic theology as interpreted through the Scotist and Ockhamist traditions. Major was a significant conciliarist theologian. He believed in the supreme authority of a general council of the church over the pope, with the foundational assumption that constitutional law is for the benefit of the people, rather than for the pleasure of the ruler.[10] As we shall later see, this conciliar, constitutional thought would become very important in the approach of Calvin, and even more so in that of his French Huguenot and Scots followers. In this regard, Major's *History of Greater Britain* became (especially after the time of Calvin) a much mined treasure store for both the late sixteenth-century Reformers and Roman Catholic Counter-Reformation scholars, united in a desire to find historical examples of people deposing unjust kings within a framework of constitutive law and custom.

In the more strictly theological sphere, Calvin seems to have been deeply influenced by Major's hostility to medieval allegorical interpretations of Scripture in favor of "the literal interpretation." In the words of T. F. Torrance:

> The literal sense is essential, for it is upon it alone that we can build doctrine. . . . That is why it is so important to take account of the scope of the Scriptures and to square every passage with the context, not only with the immediate context of the passage in question, but with the whole context of the Gospel. . . . The literal sense is achieved through contextual and comparative exegesis, for that establishes the real as distinct from a merely accidental . . . meaning.[11]

Of course, Calvin's exegetical work was to become far more indebted to the Northern European Christian Humanist Renaissance thinkers, such as Guillaume Bude, Lefevre d'Etaples, and Erasmus. But undoubtedly Major opened the way that Calvin followed (and Major rejected) into the critical historico-literary, linguistic interpretation of texts developed by the "Revival of Learning." Renaissance man that Calvin in certain respects was, his learning at the feet of John Major anchored him into the Catholic tradition in his scriptural interpretation long after he had formally broken with the Roman Church, as any reading of his *Institutes of the Christian Religion, Tracts and Treatises*, and *Commentaries* will show. For Calvin as for Major:

> Interpretation takes place properly only within the context and history of the Church's tradition. The understanding of the Scriptures must be "squared" with the decisions of the councils, the teaching of the great doctors of the past . . . especially through the work of the fathers and councils. . . .[12]

Calvin's theology and statesmanship are marked in one other significant way by the example and teaching of Major, for which Major was indebted to Duns Scotus: theology is a *scientia practica*.[13] The practical rather than speculative nature of theology was to involve Calvin in a plethora of activities and controversies that Major could scarcely have dreamed of.

Calvin's skills as an interpreter of ancient texts were to be keenly refined when, at the behest of his father, who decided his son must study law rather than prepare for the priesthood, Calvin left Paris for the University of Orleans in about 1528. He studied there under Pierre de l'Etoile, "the keenest jurisconsul of all the doctors of France" in the estimation of Beza (the successor of Calvin at Geneva).[14] Then in 1529 Calvin moved to the University of Bourges to hear the lectures of the brilliant Italian legal scholar Andrea Alciati, who was also an accomplished humanist.[15]

L'Etoile was continuing in the older tradition of teaching Roman law on the basis of Justinian's *Pandecta* and with the assistance of Accursius's *Glossa Magna*, with the assumption that modern problems could be handled by reference to details and principles drawn from this thousand-year-old code. Alciati on the other hand attacked this approach, for as Skinner states:

> As the immediate applicability of Justinian's Code began to appear increasingly problematic, it no longer seemed at all obvious that the essence of any proper legal training ought to consist of glossing the contents of the Code and applying the results directly to prevailing circumstances. . . . The basic aim ought rather to be that of studying the history and development of the indigenous laws and customs of one's own country.[16]

As Calvin's early letters show, he definitely preferred l'Etoile, and yet he was marked by Alciati. Torrance says of his debt to the latter, ". . . he was nevertheless indebted to him for initiating him into research into the classical and cultural sources of legal and social institutions and in reinforcing the need for a purer Latinity and a better literary taste."[17] Calvin drew something more from Alciati and l'Etoile that reinforced his Scotist commitment to a combination of the theoretical and the practical (i.e., *scientia practica*).

> . . . perhaps the most important thing that Calvin learned from l'Etoile and Alciati was the danger of a schism in legal science between theory and practice, and between rhetoric and logic, and that abstract formalism among humanists must be avoided as much as among scholastics.[18]

Perhaps even more important to Calvin than his legal studies, in both Orleans and Bourges, was his fuller exposure to the Humanist

Revival of Learning and to currents of Lutheranism. He studied Greek under the German Melchior Wolmar, who was by this time a Lutheran. Soon after coming to Bourges, and perhaps owing to his personal freedom of choice after the death of his father, Calvin returned to Paris in order to pursue literary studies at the College Royal—an institution founded by King Francis I and encouraged by the great humanist Bude. There he continued his studies in Greek under Danes and commenced Hebrew under Vatable.

Calvin was all his lifetime a thinker concerned to integrate various fields of knowledge—the ultimate goal of *scientia practica*. It is clear that his drawing together of legal and literary humanist studies would raise certain questions for his now growing interest in the original texts of Scripture: "Why should not the literary and source criticism of biblical texts reveal new yet old substance as it had revealed in the study of legal texts?"[19] But before he turned in earnest to biblical exposition, Calvin wrote his first book, *A Commentary on Seneca's De Clementia*. This was in 1532, generally considered to be shortly before his conversion to evangelical Christianity.

This first published work demonstrates Calvin's reliance upon the historical, critical, and literary tools of the European Renaissance, especially as used by Erasmus, Bude, and Valla. Wendel writes:

> In reading his *Commentary* one can hardly refrain from comparisons with the method used in the *Paraphrases* of Erasmus, and above all in the *Annotations* of Guillaume Bude on the *Pandecta*. Like Bude, Calvin begins with a rather long philological explanation, he appeals to grammar and logic, he points out the figures of rhetoric, draws upon his knowledge of antiquity to collect parallel quotations from other ancient writers and from Seneca himself.[20]

Calvin Becomes Protestant

Wendel,[21] T. H. L. Parker,[22] and others have shown that later and after his conversion, Calvin "further refined this method and applied it to the Scriptures themselves." The acceptance of this Calvinian method of integrating humanist literary, historico-critical methodology with research into the meaning of the scriptural texts continues to this day among Christian and Jewish scriptural exegetes of various theological persuasions.

> True, Valla had already employed the humanist method in his *Annotations* upon the New Testament and Erasmus was following him along that path: but it was Calvin who first made it the very basis of his exegesis and in doing so founded the modern science of exegetics.[23]

Calvin's ability to handle ancient texts and his integrative mode of thinking when later joined to his newly found evangelical faith caused him to be continually sought out by others as a teacher (as he himself later wrote).[24] In spite of his natural shyness and his desire to live a life of scholarly quietude,[25] he was now marked out as "... a man of action and he could not draw back into a life of detached study and contemplation."[26]

Owing to Calvin's part in Nicolas Cop's Lutheran-inspired Rectoral Address at the University of Paris on All Saints' Day, 1533, he had to flee to avoid prosecution by the authorities. His flight from France would become a permanent one after "the affair of the placards" in October of 1534, in which "Lutheran" placards were posted in public places, provoking strong reaction by the religious and civil authorities, who saw it as seditious activity. After visits in various directions, and having experienced firsthand persecution by the civil powers of his native land for his religious convictions, Calvin headed to Basle.

While in Basle, Calvin wrote the first edition of his monumental work (published in 1536), which he would keep revising until 1559, *The Institutes of the Christian Religion,* with its prefatory letter to Francis I of France, to which we have already referred. The historical situation Calvin addresses in this letter clearly influenced his political and theological approach for the rest of his life. Francis I was in the strange situation of persecuting the Protestants in France even while he was in league with the Protestant princes of Germany against their common rival, Emperor Charles V of the Holy Roman Empire. Thus Francis I had to give some explanation to the German princes as to why he was persecuting their fellow Protestants in his own country. His answer was simple: he depicted the French Protestants as sheer anarchists. He classed them with the Anabaptists, who, as the ruling powers at that time understood it, wished to overthrow all government (especially after the events concerning the polygamous kingdom of Munster).

Calvin of course was determined to show that true Protestants were loyal to the civil magistrate and were in no sense political revolutionaries. This desire to vindicate fellow evangelicals from the charge of political radicalism is undoubtedly part of the reason why Calvin was exceptionally conservative all of his life in strongly opposing revolutionary movements against bad rulers. As we shall see later, Calvin eagerly dissociated himself from John Knox's more radical stand for civil resistance in Scotland in the late 1550s. Calvin's thought underwent some evolution on this point in the 1560s, however, during the religious wars in France.

Calvin's Difficult Relationship with Geneva

Not only would Calvin's views on law and authority be shaped by the situation in France; they would also be filtered through the political exigencies of the republican city-state of Geneva, where in 1536 he settled as "teacher," and eventually as leading pastor. Calvin's first period of ministry in Geneva was to last for only two years because of his embroilment in the troublesome political and religious scene there. Geneva had recently and successfully revolted against its ruling Catholic bishop and his supporter, the Duke of Savoy. It then became largely dependent upon the domineering Protestant city of Berne. Geneva itself was then controlled by four "syndics" and several town councils, including a "general council," which was an assembly of all the citizens. For all practical purposes, the system tended to be one of aristocratic representation, as Williston Walker has shown.[27]

Although they had declared for the Reformation, the people of Geneva apparently wished to keep the new ecclesiastical power weak, lest they lose control over their own affairs now that they were rid of bishop and duke. The situation was also complicated by the fact that most of the reform leaders were incomers from France, of whom the native Genevans were at least somewhat suspicious. However, since Geneva had broken with Roman Catholicism, an official confession and a new ecclesiastical organization were needed. Calvin endeavored to supply this by submitting a series of articles to the town councils in January of 1537. These articles would require an official confession of faith by all of the inhabitants, which is typical of Calvin, and unlike the Anabaptists and the majority of post-eighteenth-century Protestant denominations, which held to an ecclesiastical community consisting of believers rather than of all inhabitants of a particular region. Here, as in many other significant areas, Calvin remained loyal to those aspects of the medieval Catholic tradition which were faithful to Scripture despite his formal break with the Roman ecclesiastical system, much of which he felt violated the Word of God and against which he directed a continuing polemic. Calvin and his fellow Reformers thus considered themselves to be true catholics, although not Roman Catholics.

The factor in these articles that brought controversy with the town councils to a head was Calvin's insistence (also in line with traditional Catholic practice) that the church should have the right to exclude unworthy persons from the Lord's Supper, and to excommunicate them, if necessary. Geneva, in which the civil authorities largely controlled the church, was not ready for this since they interpreted it as an interference with their power to govern public morals. These matters were put to a vote in February of 1538, and Calvin's side lost, though the controversy continued. Shortly afterward Calvin and his Reformed associates were ordered to leave town. Yet church-state relations continued to be a crucial practical, as well as theological, concern in Calvin's life.

Calvin took refuge for the next three years in the Reformed city of Strasbourg, under the tutelage of the distinguished Reformer, Martin Bucer. Bucer influenced Calvin theologically and politically as well as personally (actually helping to find a good wife for him!). While in Strasbourg Calvin led a parish of French-speaking Protestants. He also took part in a number of Lutheran-Reformed, and Protestant-Catholic colloquies, where he came to know many of the leading religious leaders of Europe, including Luther's successor, Melanchthon. He revised his *Institutes* while there (1539) and published other works.

Calvin's close contacts with the German Lutheran churches led him to criticize them on two counts. First, he felt their liturgy was too dependent upon Catholic tradition and not sufficiently reformed according to scriptural principles. Even more importantly, as Wendel states, ". . . his ideal of a Church, not independent of the State, but autonomous and free to act in its own sphere, came into conflict at every instant with the strict dependency to which the German Churches were subjected by the political power. . . ."[28]

By 1541 the political situation had changed in Geneva so that Calvin was invited back to take charge once again of the Reformed church in that troubled city. He would remain there until the end of his life in 1564. As the price for his returning, the city authorities had to indicate their willingness for him once more to draft constitutional regulations by which the church was to be guided, for—as he wrote to Farel—"the church cannot stand firm unless a government is constituted as prescribed to us by the Word of God and observed in the early church."[29] Out of this came Calvin's *Ecclesiastical Ordinances*, adopted by the general council of the citizens in November of 1541.

The central issue of this legislation was that of the church's authority to act in its own proper sphere, free from the control of the civil magistrate (though not totally independent of it). The church's freedom in its own house was centered in its right to excommunicate spiritual offenders from ecclesiastical privileges. Calvin insisted that the church, rather than the town council, should have this right.[30] He won his point, but only in a limited sense. The final text of the *Ordinances* was so ambiguous that the civil authorities left open the door for continued interference by the town council in church discipline.[31] It took nearly fifteen more years of often bitter controversy between the Geneva Reformed ministers and the civil magistrate to establish the church's right of spiritual discipline (with the ultimate authority of excommunication).

The ecclesiastical details of these *Ordinances* need not concern us. Calvin borrowed from Martin Bucer his four orders of ministry:[32] pastors, teachers, elders, and deacons. Yet two points, however, do require comment. First, Calvin still allowed the civil magistrate the authority to adjudicate doctrinal controversies among the ministers,[33] "which indicates that he had no belief in full independence of church from state." Second, Calvin set up something essentially new in Reformed Protestantism (as John T. McNeill has pointed out[34]): the consistory, or church session, which was to have the authority to determine fitness for admission to the Lord's Supper. The consistory was formed of both ministers and lay elders approved by the town council. Severe tensions periodically surfaced between the church consistory and the town council over their respective jurisdictions, especially in various controversies coming to a head in the elections of 1548 and 1553. These elections were lost by the partisans of Calvin and his consistory, but when the supporters of Calvin later won the elections of 1555, the issue was settled in favor of the spiritual authority of the session to discipline offenders.

Although these elections of 1555 finally gave the Calvin party preponderant control, Geneva did not become then, nor was it ever, a theocracy. As Wendel has ably stated:

> . . . one could no more speak of an annexation of the Church by the Magistracy than of a preponderance of the Church over the civil power. The distinction between the two powers was the foundation of the entire edifice. Each of these autonomous powers, State and Church, was conceived as issuing from the Divine will. . . . it is therefore inaccurate to speak, as people often do, of a theocratic confusion of powers. . . . each power had, theoretically at least, its well-defined domain.[35]

Basil Hall once pointed out that far from being a theocratic dictator, "Calvin in Geneva had less power either in theory or in practice than had Archbishop Whitgift in England, and less again than had Archbishop Laud, or Cardinal Richelieu in France, for he had neither the authority of their office nor the consistent and powerful political support which they received."[36] Though even after 1555 Geneva did not become a theocracy, it was thereafter looked upon by its ministers as a much more Christian city. This was so especially after the 1561 revision of the *Ecclesiastical Ordinances*, which strengthened the consistory while safeguarding "the distinction shown to us in the Holy Scripture between the sword and authority of the Magistrate, and the superintendence that the Church should exercise, to bring all Christians to the obedience and true service of God."[37] Various scholars have noted that "the distinction and yet the close union of Church and State which Calvin achieved with the precision possible in the self-governing city state was an important factor in the spread of Calvinism."[38]

Calvin's Belief in "Two Kingdoms"

Underlying the long years of struggle to establish authority in the consistory lay Calvin's view that "the two powers, civil and religious, ought to be complementary"[39] and that "minister and magistrate seem to be the parallel officers of a body at once ecclesiastical and political."[40] As Calvin wrote in a letter of 24 October 1538:

> As the magistrate ought by punishment and physical restraint to cleanse the church of offenses, so the minister of the Word should help the magistrate in order that fewer may sin. Their responsibilities should be so joined that each helps rather than impedes the other.[41]

Calvin wrote at some length in his *Institutes* on the concept of "two kingdoms," civil and spiritual. He dealt with the purposes, parts, and forms of civil government, the various types and uses of law, and the limitations of civil authority. Throughout these discussions he constantly related civil government and law to the spiritual realm. In his pivotal twentieth chapter of Book 4 of the *Institutes*, Calvin begins by asserting that man is under a twofold government: civil and spiritual. He states that while "Christ's spiritual kingdom and the civil jurisdiction are things completely distinct,"[42] Gospel freedom by no means liberates men from the proper control of civil magistrates. Unlike what he understood the Anabaptists to be saying,[43] Calvin denied that "the whole nature of government is a thing polluted." Rather, "civil government has as its appointed end, so long as we live among men, to cherish and protect the outward worship of God, to defend sound doctrine of piety and the position of the church, to adjust our life to the society of men, to form our social behavior to civil righteousness, to reconcile us with one another, and to promote general peace and tranquility" (4.20.2).

Calvin then classified civil government into three parts: "the magistrate, who is the protector and guardian of the laws; the laws, according to which he governs; the people, who are governed by the laws and obey the magistrate (4.20.3). Referring particularly to Romans 13:1-4, Calvin makes clear that the magistrate is ordained by God (4.20.4) and that it is anarchic for Christians to reject the magistracy owing to its coercive character (4.20.5, 7). Magistrates are responsible for maintaining "both tables of the Law" (4.20.9), which includes fostering piety. To carry out their duties, force may be necessary and appropriate (4.20.10), even war (4.20.11), and of course taxes (4.20.13).

Clemy Vautier has remarked that unlike both St. Thomas Aquinas and the later Huguenot theorists such as Beza (whom we shall consider in our next chapter), Calvin devotes no attention to the question of the legitimacy of the establishment of any particular civil form of government. (In contrast the Huguenots claimed legitimacy for a government insofar as it was founded in the consent of the people).[44] For Calvin, even if a civil order were established by force, one is not absolved from obedience to it. In the words of Cheneviere, "In the very place where the superficial observer sees only the fortuitous game of someone's ambition or of merely human courage or weakness, the believer ought to recognize the hand of God—even in those affairs which strike him as the most unjust" (my translation).[45] Calvin's interpretation of the meaning of Romans 13 and I Peter 2:13f. on this point is succinctly summarized by Vautier:

> Since St. Paul teaches that the Power is ordained by God, that magistrates are established by him, submission is thus due to them—pure and simple. The very existence of the Power gives it the right to demand obedience. This is the source of all actual legitimate authority. (My translation.)[46]

While not concentrating on the human origins of civil government, Calvin does briefly notice three major forms of civil orders: monarchy, aristocracy, and democracy (4.20.8). While admitting the legitimacy of all, he does state his preference: "I will not deny that aristocracy, or a system compounded of aristocracy and democracy, far excels all others." Bohatec suggests that Calvin has derived this combination of a nonhereditary aristocracy-democracy from Aristotle's *Politics*,[47] but that the reason he prefers it is biblical or theological: man is a fallen creature and abuses power.

> Therefore, men's fault or failing causes it to be safer and more bearable for a number to exercise government, so that they may help one another, teach and admonish one another; and if one asserts himself unfairly, there may be a number of censors and masters to restrain his willfulness (4.20.8).

Calvin deals with the abusive propensities of monarchs in detail in his Sermon XXIX on I Samuel 8:11-22:

> For as Scripture teaches us, a well-constituted republic is a singular benefit of God, while on the other hand, a disordered state with wicked rulers and perverters of law is a sign of divine wrath against us. . . .
>
> Thus even though the world today is inundated with a flood of impiety and iniquity, let us not wonder if we see so much plundering and robbery of people everywhere, and kings and princes thinking they deserve everything they want, simply because no one opposes them.[48]

In his sermons on II Samuel (preached in 1562, during the period of the religious wars in his native France), Calvin paints a most unflattering portrait of kings and their corrupt courtesans.[49] In Sermon XIV, he states, concerning David's many wives: "Beyond the fact that he committed adultery for its own sake, was the customary attitude of princes that they ought to be privileged to do wrong above everyone else." Sermon 18 says: "Pride blinds [princes] so totally that they think they ought to be put in the rank of God."

This sober Calvinian assessment of fallen man's propensity to seize, increase, and abuse power for personal ends rather than for the welfare of the many would be developed and applied far more systematically by Calvin's heirs in France, Scotland, and colonial America, as we shall see in later chapters. Governmental principles for consent of the governed, and separation and balance of powers are all logical consequences of a most serious and Calvinian view of the biblical doctrine of the fall of man. But some generations would pass before these consequential concepts were clearly drawn out and defined, under the impact of varying historical circumstances and intellectual currents.

Calvin's ideal of an aristocratic democracy—involving the many in order to limit the inevitable tendency to abusive misrule by the one—seems to owe something to the Old Testament practice of electing kings. In his commentary on Micah 5:5, he takes the term "shepherds" in the sense of civil authorities, and notes:

> For the condition of the people most to be desired is that in which they create their shepherds by general vote (*communibus suffragiis*). For when anyone by force usurps the supreme power, that is tyranny. And where men are born to kingship, this does not seem to be in accordance with liberty. Hence the prophet says: we shall set up princes for ourselves; that is, the Lord will not only give the Church freedom to breathe, but also to institute a definite and well-ordered government, and establish this upon the common suffrages of all.[50]

He pursues this theme in his sermon on I Samuel 8:11-22, where he discusses at length the utter foolishness of the Israelites in rejecting decentralized government by patriarchal elders for a hereditary monarchy: "Well, a formerly free people who sought royal dominance and subjected themselves willingly to it and thus gave up their liberty really deserves no better."[51] Calvin's desire for an elective, representative, republican type of government, was certainly influenced by his many years of writing and preaching on the Old Testament. The regular practice (especially in the Northern Kingdom) of popular elections and deposition of kings in view of a higher "covenant" with God defined, bound, and limited civil power and human relationships within the theocratic, Israelite community. Local Old Testament rule by councils of patriarchal elders "sitting in the village gate," as well as the prototypical council of seventy elders raised up to help Moses in the wilderness, undoubtedly entered Calvin's thought about proper civil polity. He was also heavily influenced by the Swiss experience of what Harold Berman has called "the communitarian character" of urban law, which developed after the rise of Western European cities in the twelfth century and following. These biblical and more recent historical events implied "that political power was ultimately vested in the whole body of citizens."[52] And as Bouwsma states:

> He shared the civic humanists' hatred of the Roman Empire for subverting the Republic, and he drew from Augustine the character-

ization of "almost all large kingdoms" as "great robberies." Such views were closely related to the actual pluralism of contemporary Europe.[53]

Yet Calvin in his writings did not systematically develop the implications of this power in the people for representative, elective principles of civil government any more than he had done with the implications for civil government of the fact of man's fallenness. His French Huguenot successors, however, and others after them, were to pursue this, and thus would be opened an important chapter in modern political history.

Calvin's View of Law

After his discussion of the magistrate (whether of monarchical, aristocratic, or democratic appointment), Calvin moves on to discuss the law by which the magistrate is to rule the people. He discusses first "the law of God published by Moses" and then the "common laws of nations." He follows Aquinas (*Summa Theologiae* I IIae lxxxix 4) in dividing the Mosaic legislation into moral, ceremonial, and judicial laws (*Institutes* 4.20.14), holding that "there is in them that pertains to us, and what does not." The moral law is the only one of the three types with abiding validity. It is

> . . . contained under two heads, one of which simply commands us to worship God with pure faith and piety; the other, to embrace men with sincere affection. Accordingly, it is the true and eternal rule of righteousness, prescribed for men of all nations and times, who wish to conform their lives to God's will. For it is his eternal and unchangeable will that he himself be indeed worshipped by us all, and that we love one another (4.20.15).

The moral law is summarized in the Ten Commandments and in the law of love (Lev. 19:18; Deut. 6:5; Matt. 22:37-39). In *Institutes* 2.8.1 Calvin speaks of the moral law as "that inward law . . . engraved upon the hearts of all" which "asserts the very same things that are to be learned from the two Tables." He then explains that this moral law is "natural" to all humanity in that it is engraved on their consciences:

> For our conscience does not allow us to sleep a perpetual insensible sleep without being an inner witness and monitor of what we owe God, without holding before us the difference between good and evil and thus accusing us when we fail in our duty. But man is so shrouded in the darkness of errors that he hardly begins to grasp through this natural law what worship is acceptable to God (2.8.1).

Calvin immediately adds that because of our dullness and arrogance, "The Lord has provided us with a written law to give us a clearer witness of what was too obscure in the unwritten natural law . . ." (ibid.). Although the unwritten natural law tends to be obscure, it is still a legitimate source of civil authority, since it is divinely imprinted on the consciences of all (4.20.16). It gives rise to "equity," and "this equity alone must be the goal and rule and limit of all laws" (ibid.). This doctrine of equity is basic for Calvin's teaching that there is equal validity in different civil polities and systems of law.

He states, "Whatever laws shall be framed to that rule, directed to that goal, bound by that limit, there is no reason why we should disapprove of them, howsoever they may differ from the Jewish law, or among themselves" (4.20.16). In other words, Calvin denies that the whole Old Testament Jewish legislation is or should be binding on the civil polity of all nations:

> For there are some who deny that a commonwealth is duly framed which neglects the political system of Moses, and is ruled by the common laws of nations. Let other men consider how perilous and seditious this notion is; it will be enough for me to have proved it false and foolish (4.20.14).

Thus non-Judaic forms of legislation are legitimate for other countries:

> . . . every nation is left free to make such laws as it foresees to be profitable for itself. Yet these must be in conformity to that perpetual rule of love (4.20.15).

That which is universally binding is the basic principle of equity summarized in the Ten Commandments and the law of love, revealed in writing to the Jews and in the conscience to all others. Calvin asserts that the other two basic types of Old Testament law, ceremonial and judicial, are no longer binding on any country. The ceremonial has been fulfilled in the person and work of Christ (4.20.15 and 2.7.16) and the judicial is not authoritative on the nations since the general principle of equity underlying it has to be adapted to differing situations and differing times. "Therefore, as ceremonial laws could be abrogated while piety remained safe and unharmed, so too, when these judicial laws were taken away, the perpetual duties and precepts of love could still remain" (4.20.15).

In *Institutes* 4.20.16, Calvin gives examples of legitimate variations in the criminal laws among the nations. These variations do not have to come from the Old Testament legislation, but rather are to be an expression of the divinely given natural law. Calvin's *Commentary on Romans* (1:21-22; 2:14-15) deals in more detail with the divine imprinting of the natural law on men's hearts.[54] Thus, with Calvin, positive law of the various nations is more directly related to his conception of natural law than it is to Old Testament legislation. But lest we misinterpret Calvin's teaching on natural law, it is important to remember the proviso of John T. McNeill:

> In all this Calvin has no notion of modern secular interpretations of natural law. It is part of the divine endowment of the natural man, impaired indeed, but not obliterated by sin, evident in common concepts of justice and in the inner voice of conscience.[55]

Calvin would have found unthinkable the statement of Hugo Grotius in the *Prolegomena* to his *De Iure Belli ac Pacis* (1625), that "the legal principles so identified [as natural law] would have a degree of validity even if there were no God."[56] As Francis Lyall points out, Grotius meant that even apart from the assumption of the existence of God: "Reason would deduce such principles from a consideration of the nature of man, and from his need of society. Others acted on that observation, and drove a wedge between 'natural law' and any religious source. This was not, however, a sudden or a complete change of emphasis."[57]

Other Reformers such as Bucer[58] and Pierre Viret, Calvin's ministerial colleague in Lausanne,[59] maintained rather a closer connection between specific Old Testament legislation (especially "civil") and the positive law of nations, and many Puritans, such as John Cotton of England and then New England would later do the same.[60] And in a recent study of the teaching on God's law in Calvin's thought, Jean Carbonnier argued that Calvin's thinking on the subject of law developed toward a more positive view of the continuing validity of Old Testament judicial law.[61] Carbonnier holds that this development is demonstrated in Calvin's sermons on Deuteronomy (preached from 1555).

Carbonnier quotes as an instance Calvin's discussion of the Jubilee year (in his second sermon on Deuteronomy chapter XV, C.O. XXVI1, 315): "Hence we see that this law, although it was particularly binding on Israel when they were under its servitude, still today contains a doctrine which is very useful for us." Citing a number of other passages in these sermons,[62] Carbonnier summarizes by stating that by the mid 1550s, Calvin believed that the judicial laws of Moses "constituted a supplement to (natural) law towards which (positive) law should properly tend to move."[63] He comments that article 25 of the *Confession of La Rochelle* (1559), which was strongly influenced by Calvin, includes this same emphasis on the usefulness of "the ceremonies and figures of the law" for daily life, although their actual practice ceased with the coming of Christ.[64]

Although Calvin may well have developed a new emphasis by the late 1550s on the practical usefulness of Old Testament legislation, it is very doubtful that he changed his mind on the essentials. For if he had, there would have been time to have rewritten the relevant sections in his final revision of his *Institutes* in 1559 (which he did not). In short, Calvin negates the continuing obligation of Old Testament judicial and ceremonial law; yet, unlike Martin Luther, he holds a very positive view of the value of the moral law for the Christian life and for all human life.

Calvin mentioned three uses of the moral law: First, by showing us God's righteousness, it condemns our sinfulness and drives us to Christ (2.7.6, 8, 9). Second, by causing fear of punishment, it restrains evil men from sin (2.7.10, 11). And third, it is a positive guide for the Christian life (2.7.12). For Luther, the condemning function of the law is its chief use, whereas for Calvin, its condemnation is " 'accidental' to its true purpose,"[65] which is positive guidance to the Christian.

This emphasis on the "third use" of the law gives the only proper context in which we may interpret Calvin's lifelong concern with both ultimate authority and proximate legal structures: it is to restore fallen man back into the image of God for the glory of Christ. Thus Calvin says in his section on "the sum of the law":

> Now it will not be difficult to decide the purpose of the whole law; the fulfillment of righteousness to form human life to the archetype of divine purity. For God has so depicted his character in the law that if any man carries out in deeds whatever is enjoined there, he will express the image of God, as it were, in his own life (2.8.51).

The ultimate purpose of the law is the same as the ultimate purpose of all institutions of both "spiritual" and "civil" realms: to glorify God, who is the source of all law, authority, and grace, by redeeming man in Christ. That is why in Calvin's view of society, the church is so central. Without a grasp of this centrality of church and redemption we cannot understand the agenda that motivates his particular approach to various types of law and polity. Nor can we understand the powerful sway that his approach to church and state exercised on his own generation and generations to come.

The Centrality of the Church in Society

Ronald S. Wallace has explained the centrality of the church and of redemption in Christ for Calvin's approach to human politics and society in general:

> Calvin believed that what happens when humanity is redeemed in Christ gives us a true picture of what was meant to happen originally in society in its natural form. For grace always tends to reveal and restore the original form of nature. Therefore he found the ideal human order described for him in Paul's account of the Church in the New Testament. . . . In Geneva he wanted even civil society to reflect as far as it could the pattern of . . . the Church. Earthly citizenship was to be patterned on heavenly citizenship. . . .
>
> His first concern in Geneva was therefore to create at the heart

> of the city a community of the faithful in Christ whose ways of actual forbearance, love, and forgiveness would provide a pattern for the rest of civil society.[66]

Calvin believed that the responsibility the church had to Christ, its Head, determined many aspects of its relationship to the civil magistrate. The church was responsible to preach the Word of God faithfully and to administer purely the sacraments (in the Protestant view, baptism and the Lord's Supper). In the earliest sections of his *Institutes*, Calvin shows that while God has revealed himself in nature and in man's conscience, man because of his sin misinterprets and perverts this divine revelation: ". . . each one of us privately forges his own particular error . . . we forsake the one true God" (1.5.11). Thus God gives us the written Word of God so that we may truly know him. "Just as old or bleary-eyed men and those with weak vision . . . can scarcely construe two words, but with the aid of spectacles will begin to read distinctly; so Scripture, gathering up the otherwise confused knowledge of God in our minds, having dispersed our dullness, clearly shows us the true God."

Calvin immediately adds this important clause, showing the crucial relationship of Scripture, revelation, and church: "This, therefore, is a special gift, where God, to instruct the church, not merely uses a mute teacher but also opens his own most hallowed lips." (1.6.1). In other words, God himself through the preaching of his Word speaks in his church. Thus God's ultimate purpose for this world, to redeem a multitude of humanity to his image in Christ, can only be fulfilled through the church, where Scripture is preached: "Now, in order that true religion may shine upon us, we ought to hold that it must take its beginning from heavenly doctrine and that no one can get even the slightest taste of right and sound doctrine unless he be a pupil of Scripture" (1.6.2). Calvin adds that it takes the internal witness or illumination of the Holy Spirit within the human heart to convince someone of the divine truth of Scripture (1.7.4).

Calvin saw the church as the locus where Christ makes himself known to humanity (and thus redeems it to God's image) not only in the ministry of the Word, but also in the sacraments. He understood baptism and the Lord's Supper to be "signs and seals" of the vital union of believers with Christ in his death and resurrection, and with Augustine, "visible words" by which the Lord came down and made himself known afresh to his own (see 4.14-17).

Calvin's teachings that the Holy Spirit must illumine the human mind for the inspired Word to be effective within it, and that Christ himself through his Spirit comes down in the sacraments give us the proper clue to understanding his view of ministerial authority in the church and of the consequent relationship of the church to the civil order. Christ alone is the Head of the church, and his Spirit the executive agent and true worker in all ministerial action. Thus Calvin did not see ministers and elders themselves as sources of authority. Their function (although a highly honored one when properly lived out) was ministerial—to be servants of the Word of God. And for an effective ministry of the Word, they were directly dependent upon the assistance of the Holy Spirit. "All power resides in the Spirit himself," and the Lord can withdraw the Spirit when he wishes.[67] Christ blesses ministerial action while retaining full lordship and direct authority in the church in the Calvinian assessment.

J. K. S. Reid fairly summarized Calvin's viewpoint on headship and authority in the church:

> Government of the Church by the ministry of the Word, does not mean government by the ministers of the Word. As Head, Christ exercises a Lordship over the Church which does not set Him at such a distance that some kind of subordinate Lordship can arise; on the contrary, as Head He is never without the members that constitute His body: "Rule in the Church belongs to the Head Himself. Where therefore Christ is given His place, there the Church which is His body may be said to obtain the Kingdom; for Christ wishes nothing in separation from His members" (quoting *Commentary on Zechariah* 2:9).[68]

This, of course, is easier to hold in theory than to realize in practice. The difficulty lies in determining, when disagreements arise, who is faithfully expressing Christ's particular will for his church. Disagreements will arise as to points of interpretation of the Word in specific situations. Any reading of the standard biographies of Calvin will indicate the controversies, at times very bitter, that were experienced in Geneva as to the true will of God for running both church and state. Nevertheless, Calvin's revival of the concept of Christ's direct and practical headship of his church was to be a fountainhead of inspiration, controversy, and revolutionary activity—especially in Knoxian Scotland, Puritan England, and again in Covenanter Scotland in the 1680s.

No Toleration of Heresy

All of this has a most direct bearing on the limits of the authority of the civil magistrate in relationship to the church. Granted that since Christ is sole Head of the church, the magistrate is not to be in charge of ecclesiastical affairs. Yet, the magistrate, in addition to handling affairs in his own kingdom (which we have previously discussed), is also to see that the right religion is established and to prevent it "from being openly and with public sacrilege violated and defiled with impunity" (4.20.3). It is magisterial responsibility also "to remove superstitions and put an end to all wicked idolatry, to advance the kingdom of Christ and maintain purity of doctrine, to purify scandals and cleanse the filth that corrupts piety and impairs the luster of the divine majesty."[69] In summary, " No government can be happily established unless piety is the first concern . . ." (4.20.9).

Calvin here is profoundly Constantinian and medieval. He has no concept of a separation between religion and state, or of a non-Christian magistrate, or of toleration of plural churches. Drastically changing political realities and other Christian approaches (not least a widening acceptance of a number of the Anabaptist convictions on church-state separation and individual liberty) would, by the late seventeenth century cause a majority of Calvin's spiritual and political heirs increasingly to dissent from him on all of these points.

Yet we must remember that in differing with Calvin on these points, they and we today differ also with most religious leaders of his day, both Catholic and Protestant, except for the Anabaptists.

To us today it seems strange and cruel that Calvin readily consented to the official execution of the anti-Trinitarian heretic Michael Servetus by the Christian magistracy of Geneva. Much as we may deplore this sort of action, we must remember that Calvin understood the ancient Justinian Code, which prescribed the death penalty for such heresy, still to be in effect as part of the civil law. The Reformation did not purport to change this.[70] J. K. Cameron has explained, "That he [Servetus] had thereby committed an offense against the civil code of the empire accepted as legally binding on Geneva, and rendered himself guilty and subject to criminal punishment, has not, however, always been stressed."[71] We may note as well that before the collapse of Euro-communism, it was considered a crime to preach anticommunist doctrine or publicly to preach religion in much of Central and Eastern Europe.

From our twentieth-century Western perspective, then, we may now see that in these respects Calvin can be regarded as having been backward-looking rather than forward-looking so that eventually his own followers would go in another direction. But one important aspect of his teaching was (from the modern perspective) so forward-looking that not only his ecclesiastical heirs, but also much of the Western world would follow him in centuries to come without necessarily knowing it was Calvin (or for that matter any theological perspective) that they were following. That aspect was his doctrine of the limitations of all civil authority, and the people's right to resist it.

It is important to note that Calvin's teaching on this subject was not really new. His major contribution to the development of modern liberty was the emphasis he gave it in his own historical circumstances and the way he popularized it as an international ecclesiastical statesman and writer. As we shall see, what he has to say on this subject owes much to his old teacher, John Major, and to the whole post-fourteenth-century Catholic conciliar tradition, as well as to the post-Gregorian Revolution (eleventh century), with its unwitting encouragement of the development and operation of several different law spheres at the same time.[72] Calvin's teaching was indebted as well to the experience of urban law in republican city-states such as Geneva. Yet the origins of Calvin's thought at this point are not so important for us as what he actually said and the influence it had.

In defending the headship of Christ over his church, Calvin makes it clear that all human authority (whether individual or institutional) is limited; only God himself has unlimited power. On this point there was definite development in Calvin's thought over the years. As a young humanist author of the *Commentary on Seneca's De Clementia,* he followed the old Roman jurists and their later commentators, such as Ulpien, in holding that the ruler was not bound by law, *princeps legibus solutus est,* since he is the living law, *lex animata.*[73] The famous French scholar of political history, Jean Bodin would develop this old theory that the king was above the law in his *De Republica* (1576), thus helping to pave the way for absolute monarchy.[74] But while always retaining a cautious, conservative, antirevolutionary stance, Calvin came to see that the king's power is rightly limited "under law" and "under covenant."[75] Thus in the early 1560s, some thirty years after he had written his *Commentary on De Clementia,* Calvin seems to say the very opposite of *princeps legibus solutus est.*

Concerning the princes of his day (and of all times) he writes:

> This proverb has been used by tyrants for a very long time: "what matters is will, not reason." In other words they consider themselves bound by no laws. . . . Well, certainly that old saying is utterly arrogant (to go by will instead of reason), but nevertheless it is the accepted procedure in the *Institutes* of the Roman Empire. . . .
>
> For rulers judge everything to be legitimate for themselves and do not consider themselves bound by the law of God, nor do they consider his worship to pertain to themselves. Herein they are terribly mistaken. . . . Even though the power of earthly princes be great in this world, still they must realize that they are ministers and servants of God and the people.[76]

The influences toward this development in Calvin's thinking seem to have been of three sorts: (1) his continuing deep study of the Scriptures—especially of the Old Testament, which was more heavily emphasized in the Calvinist tradition than in the medieval Catholic or sixteenth-century Lutheran and Anabaptist traditions; (2) his continuing study of church history and theology—especially of the Greek and Latin Fathers; (3) the changing political situation. The Protestants in England and Scotland had suffered under the Catholic Queens Mary Tudor of England (who reigned 1553-58) and Mary Stuart of Scotland (who reigned 1560-67). The Protestants in France suffered persecution in the 1560s. Calvin moved from strong denials of sympathy with antimonarchical activity (as in his dedicatory epistle to Francis I in 1536) to openly raising the question of resistance in his early 1560s Sermon XXIX on I Samuel 8:

> . . . since kings and princes are bound by covenant to the people, to administer the law in truest equality, sincerity, and integrity; if they break faith and usurp tyrannical power by which they allow themselves everything they want: is it not possible for the people to consider together taking measures in order to remedy the evil? A difficult question indeed. . . .[77]

The Christian's Right of Resistance

Undoubtedly most of Calvin's teaching on the responsibility of the citizen toward a harsh magistrate was first modeled on Paul's command in Romans 13 to be obedient "to the higher powers," which are ordained of God.[78] This seemed to preclude resistance. And yet even from his first edition of the *Institutes* (1536), Calvin leaves a "crack in the door" for resistance to an ungodly civil order. First, he denies the right of private citizens to take the law into their own hands by taking personal vengeance against evil magistrates. Then he adds this phrase pregnant with potential influence for the future:

> For if there are now any magistrates of the people, appointed to restrain the willfulness of kings (as in ancient times the ephors were set against the Spartan kings, or the tribunes of the people against the Roman consuls, or the demarchs against the senate of the Athenians; and perhaps, as things now are, such power as the three estates exercise in every realm when they hold their chief assemblies), I am so far from forbidding them to withstand, in accordance with their duty, the fierce licentiousness of kings, that, if they wink at kings who violently fall upon and assault the lowly common folk, I declare that their dissimulation involves nefarious perfidy, because they dishonestly betray the freedom of the people, of which they know that they have been appointed protectors by God's ordinance (4.20.31, quoted from the 1559 edition, which is substantially the same as the 1536 edition).[79]

Calvin was already proclaiming the doctrine of interposition. This asserts the right and indeed, the moral duty, of lesser or "inferior" magistrates, who were between the king and the people, to take whatever action might be necessary to restrain a wicked king, or even to depose him. With Calvin's background in conciliar thinking, he would have been well aware of the rights of a general church council to depose a corrupt pope. And with his training in Roman law he would have known of the rights of the German electors to depose an emperor of the Holy Roman Empire. His ascription to lesser magistrates of an office of forcible resistance to the chief magistrate almost certainly owed something to John of Salisbury's *Policraticus* (1159) as well as to the division made by the great Romanist legal commentator, Azo (1150-1230), between "fullest" jurisdiction (belonging to the prince alone) and "less full" jurisdiction (belonging to the lesser magistrates).[80] And closer at hand were writings of Calvin's mentor, Bucer, that dealt with this subject as early as 1530.[81] There was also a similar justification of resistance in Luther's *Warning to His Dear German People* (which ran through five editions in 1531).[82] Skinner is correct in stating that "it was Luther, not Calvin, who first introduced the concept of active resistance into the political theory of the 'magisterial' Reformation."[83] But it was to be the Calvinists who most thoroughly developed and popularized the earlier conciliar, Romanist imperial and Lutheran ideas of resistance.

In later years, especially during what Skinner calls "the mid-century crisis of Protestantism,"[84] when it seemed in danger of being wiped out militarily by the forces of Catholic reaction, Calvin developed an even stronger theory of resistance than the doctrine of interposition by lesser magistrates. He appealed to the "private-law" theory of resisting evil governments, which held that an individual could resist the civil magistrate.[85] In his final Latin edition of the *Institutes* in 1559, Calvin inserted a statement to the effect that a magistrate who impiously exceeds his power thereby loses his official magisterial power, and may thus be disobeyed, for he is now no more than a private citizen (and a wrong doer at that), since—like King Darius in Daniel 6—he, "in lifting up his horns against God, had himself abrogated his power" (4.20.32).[86]

Calvin's later writings in the 1550s and 1560s show him, as

Skinner has suggested, "beginning to develop his allusions to the private-law argument into a theory of lawful opposition to tyrants."[87] He writes in his *Commentary on Acts*, (published between 1552 and 1554) that a prince or magistrate who dishonors God is reduced to nothing more than an ordinary man (chap. 4). He goes on to add in comments on chapter 17 of Acts that "we are not violating the authority of the king where our religion compels us to resist tyrannical edicts which forbid us to give Christ and God the honor and worship which is their due." He referred again to this same matter similarly in his comments on chapter 6 of his *Commentary on Daniel* (published in 1561), and he repeated and, as it were, underlined the same right to resist a demoted prince in order to obey God in his *Sermons on the Last Eight Chapters of the Book of Daniel* (published a year after his death in 1565).

Calvin, Both Conservative and Progressive

Looking back from our twentieth-century vantage point, we can see that Calvin's development of the doctrine of resistance to wicked authorities in terms of the theory of interposition by lesser magistrates and then the private-law theory was further developed and spread by his own "Calvinist" followers, by some strands of the Roman Catholic Counter-Reformation, and eventually (in a more secularized form) by Enlightenment libertarian philosophers and social theorists.[88] This was to be one of his most powerful legacies to the history of liberty in the modern Western world. Again, as with many of his other vital and seminal doctrines, he would leave the systematic development and application of it to others, many of whom we shall survey in the next four chapters. His thought on this point would be detached by others from the theological context in which it was engendered and become such a part of mainstream Western thought on political liberty and rights that its Calvinist origins would be widely forgotten.

We have noted that from our vantage point in the twentieth century, we can see the historical Calvin as both backward-looking (in terms of his denial of religious tolerance and his approval of state sanctions in support of religion) and forward-looking (in terms of the acknowledgment of divinely mandated structure and limits for all human government, including some form of consent of the governed). Where he was backward-looking, his friends as well as his enemies would within about a century and a half abandon the more intolerant aspect of his heritage and thus surpass him in a fuller practice of religious liberty. But where he was forward-looking, his thought would be amplified, systematized, and widely diffused in Western civilization. Eventually it would be modified through a disconnection from Calvin's name, from his theology, and even from Christianity itself. Thus modified, it would prevail across half of the world for nearly half a millennium.

Notes

[1] William J. Bouwsma, *John Calvin: A Sixteenth Century Portrait* (New York: Oxford University Press, 1988), p. 1.

[2] For the complex question of the date of Calvin's conversion, see Francois Wendel, *Calvin*, trans. Philip Mairet (London: Collins, 1963), pp. 37-45.

[3] See F. C. Battles's translation of Calvin's first edition of *The Institutes* (Richmond, Virginia: John Knox Press, 1975).

[4] See M. E. Cheneviere, *La Pensee Politique de Calvin* (Geneva: Slatkine, 1937) for the kind of work Calvin did in this regard.

[5] See T. F. Torrance's *The Hermeneutics of John Calvin* (Edinburgh: Scottish Academic Press, 1988) for recent work on Major's influence on Calvin, especially pp. 25-57, on "John Major of Haddington," and pp. 73-95, "The Shaping of Calvin's Mind: (A) Late Medieval Thought and Piety."

[6] Wendel, *Calvin*, pp. 16-37.

[7] Heiko O. Oberman, *The Harvest of Medieval Theology* (Cambridge: Harvard University Press, 1963).

[8] Torrance, *Hermeneutics of John Calvin*.

[9] Robert M. Kingdon, "The Control of Morals in Calvin's Geneva," in Lawrence P. Buck and Jonathan W. Zophy, eds., *The Social History of the Reformation* (Columbus, Ohio: Ohio State University Press, 1972), pp. 3-16.

[10] See Quentin Skinner, *The Foundations of Modern Political Thought* (Cambridge: Cambridge University Press, 1978), 2:43-47, 302-21.

[11] Torrance, *Hermeneutics of John Calvin*, pp. 54, 56, Major's main discussion of biblical interpretation is found in his *Commentary on the Third Book of Peter Lombard's Sentences*.

[12] Torrance, *Hermeneutics of John Calvin*, p. 57.

[13] Ibid., p. 84.

[14] See Beza's "Life of Calvin" in Calvin's *Tracts and Treatises*, 1:lxf.

[15] See Quirinius Breen, *John Calvin: A Study in French Humanism* (Grand Rapids: Eerdmans, 1931), p. 45.

[16] Skinner, *Foundations*, pp. 269, 270.

[17] Torrance, *Hermeneutics of John Calvin*, p. 99.

[18] Ibid.

[19] Ibid.

[20] Wendel, *Calvin*, p. 31.

[21] Ibid.

[22] T. H. L. Parker, *Calvin's New Testament Commentaries* (SCM Press: London, 1971).

[23] Wendel, *Calvin*, p. 96.

[24] In his introduction to his translation of the *Institutes*, F. L. Battles writes, ". . . he was surrounded by enquiries wherever he went" (p. xxxi).

[25] Calvin later wrote that Farel uttered imprecations against his wishes to avoid public service for scholarly retirement. Cf. *Commentary on Psalms*, pp. 25-26.

[26] Torrance, *Hermeneutics of John Calvin*, p. 160.

[27] Williston Walker, *John Calvin: the Organiser of Reformed Protestantism 1509-1564* (New York: Schocken Books, 1969).

[28] Wendel, *Calvin*, pp. 64, 65.

[29] Letters to Farel, September, 16th, 1541, C.O. XI, 281.

[30] See the important discussion of Calvin's reasoning here in J. Bohatec, *Calvin's Lehre von Staat und Kirche* (Breslau: M. and H. Marcus, 1937), pp. 539-63.

[31] Quoted in R. S. Wallace, *Calvin, Geneva, and the Reformation* (Edinburgh: Scottish Academic Press, 1988), I.5.2.

[32] See Wendel, *Calvin*, p. 76.

[33] See Wendel, *L'Eglise de Strasbourg, sa Constitution et son Organization, 1532-1535*, numéro 38, Etudes d'histoire et de philosophie religieuses (Paris publiés par la Faculté de Théologie protestante de l'université de Strasbourg, 1942), pp. 171ff.

[34] J. T. McNeill, *The History and Character of Calvinism* (New York: Oxford University Press, 1962) p. 151.

[35] Wendel, *Calvin*, p. 79.

[36] Basil Hall. "The Calvin Legend," in *John Calvin: Courtenay Studies in Reformation Theology*, ed. Duffield et al. (Appleford: The Sutton Courtenay Press, 1966), p. 11.

[37] C.O., Xa, 121.

[38] Wallace, *Calvin, Geneva, and the Reformation*, p. 113, referring to T. M. Parker, *Christianity and the State in the Light of History* (London: Black, 1955), p. 160.

[39] Wendel, *Calvin*, p. 309.

[40] Bouwsma, *John Calvin*, p. 217.

[41] C.O. X, 273.

[42] *Institutes* 4.20.1. The quotations will be from Battles's translation.

[43] Calvin frequently misunderstood and misrepresented the Anabaptists, as Charles M. Swezey shows in "The Significance of Calvin's Tracts Against the Anabaptists for the Church Today" in *Calvin Studies Colloquium*, J. H. Leith and C. Raynal; eds. (Davidson College, N.C., 1982), pp. 1-15. Yet Calvin was right that their negative estimates of Christian participation in civil government was profoundly different from his (and that of the ancient Catholic tradition).

[44] Clemy Vautier, *Les Theories Relatives a la Souverainete et a la Resistance chez L'auteur des Vindiciae Contra Tyrannos* (1579) (Lausanne: F. Roth, et cie 1947), pp. 61, 120, 122, 127, 130, 131, 142.

[45] "La ou le simple spectateur ne voit que le jeu d'une ambition, du courage ou de la faiblesse des hommes, le croyant doit voir la main de Dieu, meme dans ce qui lui apparait le plus injuste." Cheneviere, *La Pensee Politique de Calvin*, p. 305.

[46] "Puisque saint Paul enseigne que le Pouvoir est voulu de Dieu, que les magistrats sont etablis par lui, la soumission leur est due purement et simplement. L'existence du Pouvoir etant son titre a l'obeissance, positive et legitimite se recouvrent entierement." Vautier, *Les Theories*, p. 127.

[47] J. Bohatec, *Bude und Calvin: Studien zur Gedan kenwelt des franzosichen Fruhhumanismus* (Graz: Bohlau, 1950), p. 458.

[48] Trans. Douglas Kelly in Leith and Raynal, eds., *Calvin Studies Colloquium*, p. 67.

[49] See Douglas Kelly, "Some Aspects of the Preaching of John Calvin" in *Evangel* 5, 3 (Autumn 1987): 10f. These sermons have been published as *Sermons on 2 Samuel: Chapters 1-13*, trans. Douglas Kelly (Edinburgh: Banner of Truth, 1992).

[50] *Corpus Reformatorum* XLIII, 374, as quoted in J. T. McNeill's introduction to John Calvin, *On God and Political Duty*, Library of Liberal Arts, vol. 23 (Indianapolis: Bobbs-Merrill, 1956), pp. xxii, xxiii.

[51] Trans. Kelly in Leith and Raynal, eds., *Calvin Studies Colloquium*, p. 67.

[52] Harold Berman, *Law and Revolution: The Formation of the Western Legal Tradition* (Cambridge, Mass.: Harvard University Press, 1983), p. 397.

[53] Bouwsma, *John Calvin*, p. 208.

[54] For Calvin's views of natural law, see John T. McNeill, "Natural Law in the Teaching of the Reformation," *Journal of Religion* 26 (1946): 179-82; J. Bohatec, *Calvin und das Recht* (Aalen: Serentia, 1971), pp. 3-32 and his Calvin's *Lehre von Staat und Kirche*, pp. 20-35, and Wendel, *Calvin*, pp. 206-8.

[55] McNeill in his introduction to Calvin, *On God and Political Duty*, pp. xvi, xvii. While relying heavily on St. Paul (in Rom. 1 and 2) Calvin's thought on natural law was almost certainly influenced by St. Thomas. Scholars have long posited a Stoic element in Calvin's natural law theory (e.g. Wendel, *Calvin*, pp. 33-34), but less research has been done on the Thomist elements in Calvin.

[56] Paraphrased by Francis Lyall, "The Influence of the Bible on Law," in an article yet to be published in *The Oxford Companion to the Bible*, ed. Bruce Metzger and Michael Coogan (New York: Oxford University Press), p. 9.

[57] Ibid., pp. 9, 10.

[58] See Bucer's introduction to *De Regno Christi* and Wilhelm Pauck, "Martin Bucer's Conception of a Christian State" in *Princeton Theological Review* 2, 6 (1928): 80-88.

[59] See Robert Dean Linder, *The Political Ideas of Pierre Viret* (Geneva: Librairie Droz, 1964), pp. 55, 61, 63, 65, 86, 94, 103.

[60] See Cotton's Moses, *His Judicials*, reprinted in *The Journal of Christian Reconstruction* (Winter 1975-76): 117-28.

[61] Jean Carbonnier, "Droit et Theologie chez Calvin," in *Coligny ou les sermons imaginaires: Lectures pour le Protestantisme Francais d'aujourd'hui* (Paris: Presses Universitaires de France, 1970), pp. 39-51.

[62] See "Droit et Theologie chez Calvin," pp. 45, 46.

[63] Ibid., p. 45.

[64] Ibid.

[65] *Institutes* 2.7.1 n. 1 (p. 348).

[66] Wallace, *Calvin, Geneva, and the Reformation*, p. 117.

[67] Calvin, *Commentary on Malachi*, 4:6.

[68] Reid in *Service in Christ*, ed. J. I. McCord and T. H. L. Parker (Grand Rapids: Eerdmans, 1966), 102.

[69] Calvin, *Commentary on Isaiah*, 49:23.

[70] Our twentieth-century perspective, it must be added, is generally more comfortable criticizing the sixteenth-century execution of some hundreds of heretics than dealing with our own society's abortion of millions of infants.

[71] J. K. Cameron, "Scottish Calvinism and the Principles of Intolerance" in *Reformatio Perennis: Essays on Calvin and the Reformation*, ed. Gernish and Benedetto (Pittsburgh: Pickwick Press, 1981), p. 114. See his note 6 on pp. 125, 126.

[72] See Berman, *Law and Revolution*.

[73] *Digeste*, 1, 3, 32. See the Hugo and Battles edition of Calvin's *De Clementia Commentary*, The Renaissance Society of America, Renaissance Text Series, 3 (Leiden: E. J. Brille, 1969).

[74] J. Bodin, *De Republica*, 2nd ed., Latin, (1586), 7:84.

[75] See Sermon XXIX on I Samuel, trans. Kelly, in *Calvin Studies Colloquium*, p. 66.

[76] Ibid., pp. 67, 69.

[77] Ibid., p. 66.

[78] Cheneviere, *La Pensee Politique de Calvin*, p. 325.

[79] See Skinner, *Foundations*, pp. 206-24.

[80] Berman, *Law and Revolution*, pp. 288-94.

[81] Justification of armed resistance was added by Bucer into his *Explications of the Four Gospels*, first published in 1527, see Skinner, *Foundations*, p. 205.

[82] See Skinner, *Foundations*, p. 201.

[83] Ibid., p. 206.

[84] Ibid., p. 219.

[85] See Skinner on the "Private Law Theory," ibid., pp. 217-24.

[86] It is possible that Calvin was influenced by the widely heralded *Confession of Magdeburg* of 1550 (Skinner, *Foundations*, p. 207), which ties together both the doctrines of interposition and the "private-law" theory as Skinner shows (pp. 207-11). It is certain that Calvin's follower, Knox, was influenced by it, for he quotes it in his *History of the Reformation in Scotland* 2:127-34. See Battles's translation of *Institutes*, p. 1519 n. 54.

[87] Skinner, *Foundations*, p. 220.

[88] See ibid., pp. 230ff.

2

Calvinism in France: The Huguenot Experience

SINCE ITS INCEPTION in the 1540s, Calvinism remained a minority view in France and was largely suppressed by the time of the revocation of the Edict of Nantes in 1685 (which had since given the Protestants official legal protection). Yet the Protestant or Huguenot minority developed a carefully articulated theory of religious and political liberties (at least in the areas of thought and practice that concerned them) in light of its difficult position *vis a vis* the Catholic French State. Its viewpoint both radicalized and, in a few areas, systematized ideas of the more restrained John Calvin. Ironically it had far wider influence beyond France (in the Netherlands, Scotland, England, and the American colonies) than in its native land. Perhaps its most potent influence would be cloaked under other names than Calvinism. Teaching on the derived sovereignty of the people, and their inherent right to resistance, would pass (indirectly and combined with ideas of very different parentage) into late seventeenth-century English political theories of human rights. Again it would pass into similar eighteenth-century American debates on law and government, by this time somewhat detached from the Calvinist theological context.

The Huguenots: An Influential Minority in France

Estimates of Huguenot strength in the late sixteenth century vary greatly, from as few as 5 percent to as much as 25 percent of the French population. It was stronger in some areas than others, especially strong in Normandy, Poitou, and parts of Languedoc. The Huguenots had considerable support among some of the high nobility and were especially favored among intellectuals and the rising middle class. The French government, however, saw Protestantism as a serious threat to the authority of the crown and the unity of the state, which was based on traditional Catholicism. Later events would show that this fear was not entirely ungrounded.

At first, especially before the outbreak of the religious wars in France in 1562, the Huguenot theorists were, like their teacher Calvin in Geneva, eager to demonstrate their loyalty to the French government and their antirevolutionary credentials. Even at the beginning of the religious wars, the Huguenot leader, the Prince de Conde, argued that his troops had entered Paris to protect the queen regent and her son, the king, who were alleged to be in captivity to the strongly Catholic Guise faction (of which family the queen regent of Scotland, mother of Mary Stuart, was a member).[1]

John Calvin had publicly expressed disapproval of any revolutionary action of his fellow Protestants at that stage of affairs (the late 1550s and early 1560). He specifically distanced himself from *The First Blast of the Trumpet Against the Monstrous Regiment of Women* by his Scottish disciple, John Knox.[2] Calvin's assistant (and later, successor) in Geneva, Theodore Beza, had also dissociated himself from the "Conspiracy of Amboise" (an unsuccessful and inept Protestant attempt to kidnap King Francis II in 1560). In a letter of 16 April 1561, John Calvin told the great Hugeunot leader of France, Admiral de Coligny, how often he had been asked, "Is it not legitimate for the children of God to resist oppressive tyranny?" Calvin's reply was that if the believers shed one drop of blood, then whole rivers would inundate Europe. "Thus," reasoned Calvin, "it would be better for all of us to perish at once than to expose the name of Christianity and the Gospel to such shame." The Huguenots clearly hoped to placate the more moderate Catholics, and especially the royal family, who were not of the fiercely anti-Protestant "Holy League" faction led by the politically ambitious Guise family. And, it must be added, most Huguenots probably remained sincere royalists and essentially antirevolutionary throughout the changing events of the sixteenth century in line with the confessions to which they gave credence (as article 39 of the Gallican Confession, article 36 of the Belgic Confession, and article 30 of the Second Helvitic Confession).[3]

The French Protestants had taken up arms after the massacre of a congregation of Huguenots during a worship service at Vassy in March of 1562. A reformed church had already been officially organized (in secret) at Paris in 1559 during the meeting of the Protestant national synod there. Presbyterian polity (which would soon be emulated in Scotland) was set up, beginning with the lowest judicatories of local church consistories (or sessions in Scotland) composed of representative elders, on to middle or regional judicatories (called presbyteries in Scotland) composed of elders sent from the church consistories in that district, and finally to the highest judicatory, the national synod (general assembly in Scotland) composed of elders sent from the regional presbyteries. The office of elder included both clergy (ministers) and representative lay leadership.

The first national synod was composed of representatives from "more than sixty of the one hundred churches that could then be counted in France."[4] The synod adopted a confession of faith, which came from a draft of thirty-five articles prepared by Calvin, and a rule of discipline, which drew from Calvin's *Institutes*, as well as the experience of the churches influenced by Bucer in Strasbourg.

This Gallican Confession, in line with Calvin, taught the supreme authority of Scripture as being from God alone. That belief would later strongly undergird the Huguenot resistance against the pro-Catholic French Monarchy. In 1571 the Seventh National Synod adopted this confession at La Rochelle. As an affirmation of the transcendent authority of God's written Word over all human arrangements, it proved to be an important foundational document for them. It gave the Huguenot minority comfort and strength in the assertion of the doctrine of eternal election of specific persons to salvation regardless of human circumstances and considerations, as well as the doctrine of God's total providential control of all events.

Even evil events and seeming disasters are to be seen as beneficently and sinlessly used by God for the ultimate good of his elect people. Such a confessional teaching gave constancy to a minority facing almost insurmountable odds, humanly speaking.

After 1567 the Huguenots had not only to face the fervently Catholic Guise faction, but also the more moderate Catholics. In that year the queen regent, Catherine de Medicis, took up arms against the Protestant forces of the Prince de Conde, who had previously proclaimed himself her "protector." It became increasingly difficult to assume an antirevolutionary and promonarchical stance. It was impossible to do so after Catherine approved of the massacre of tens of thousands of Protestants in Paris and elsewhere on Saint Bartholomew's Eve in August of 1572. This carnage plunged France once again into civil war, with entire areas such as Languedoc, and port cities such as La Rochelle claiming independence from the monarchical government in Paris.

Huguenot Revolutionary Tracts

As far as the development of political thought is concerned, the most important thing to come out of these struggles was a group of Protestant tracts justifying revolution on an old yet new basis. They taught concepts of religious liberty flowing from a divinely ordained covenant structure of society, as well as a concept of popular sovereignty, giving the people of the nation power to make and depose kings. Although the Protestants lost the struggle militarily, these concepts became internationally influential long after the fight for freedom was lost within the French nation. The Huguenot thought on these matters was developed in a series of major "tracts for the times" after 1572.

Skinner has summarized two key moral-political problems the Huguenots addressed in these writings: first, the need to legitimate their revolution against the constituted government in the eyes of their own followers; and second, the need to provide "a more constitutionalist and less purely sectarian ideology of opposition" in order "to broaden the basis of their support" among moderate Catholics to oppose the Valois monarchy.[5]

Francois Hotman, who managed to escape the Saint Bartholomew massacre and fled to the safety of Geneva in late 1572, wrote the first of the three major Huguenot tracts that will concern us in this chapter. He published *Francogallia* in 1573 (and a second expanded edition in 1576). Unlike many other Huguenot (and Scottish Reformed) tracts, it is not written in a polemical form, but as Franklin says, "rather is a humanist investigation of French constitutional antiquities by a great scholar, who was one of the leading jurists of his age."

> In the *Francogallia*, the highly sophisticated documentary technique initially developed by the humanists to restore and interpret the sources of classical antiquity is applied to a reconstruction and illustration of the ancient public law of France.[6]

Hotman assumes that the principles of ancient constitutional tradition of France are still valid, and he uses them to critique the Valois monarchy of his day. Hotman holds that one of the major principles of the ancient French tradition is "that the king is nothing more than a magistrate for life and is constantly subject to removal by the people for violation of the duties of his office."[7] He attempts to prove this principle by demonstrating the elective nature of the early French monarchy. He documents from ancient texts "the right of the people to depose not only individual rulers but entire dynasties for incompetence or tyranny."[8] By reinterpreting feudal concepts, he argues that the historical change from election to succession by male primogeniture does not invalidate the public nature of the office "held of the people as the ultimate owner and subject to definite conditions."[9]

Another principle of the ancient constitution was held to be the public council of the realm, which he equates with the Three Estates of his own day, theoretically based on the concept of representation of the various social classes and various regions of the land. His real interest in the Three Estates (which had not functioned for years) was, in line with Calvin's doctrine of "interposition by lesser magistrates" (*Institutes* 3.20.30), "to revive their political role by reminding his contemporaries of the powers they had anciently possessed" such as electing and deposing kings.[10]

For all his quoting of ancient sources, Hotman's concern was not antiquarian. As Skinner notes, "His argument was well calculated to persuade a wide spectrum of opinion that the Valois government was acting unconstitutionally, and was thus calculated to win a broadly based and not merely a sectarian measure of support for the Huguenot revolution."[11] The mainly selective nature of his historical research was soon pointed out by royalist writers, who argued that his evidence "was frequently tendentious and inaccurate."[12] They argued that the French monarchy was not elective and that the king did not share power or *imperium* with the Estates.[13]

Hotman's tract did not sufficiently meet the needs of the Huguenots by "justifying a direct revolutionary challenge to the alleged tyranny of the existing government."[14] Others would step in the gap to provide this justification for popular revolution. The first to do so was Calvin's successor at Geneva, Theodore Beza (1519-1605), who conferred with Hotman on these pressing questions after the latter fled there in 1572.

Beza, following Calvin, had already suggested in his 1554 *Punishment of Heretics by the Civil Magistrate* that "lesser magistrates" could resist the upper magistrates to defend the true religion, and that magistrates were established by the consent of the people. But in the present desperate circumstances, Beza, after interaction with Hotman, transformed "Hotman's reflections into a general constitutionalist doctrine of the state"[15] in his *Right of Magistrates* (1574).

As Franklin and Skinner have suggested, Beza and Mornay (whom we shall presently consider), "turned to the scholastic and Roman Law traditions of radical constitutionalism."[16] Gerson, Major, Suarez, and others in the conciliarist tradition had long held the authority of the broader body—represented by a general council—to bring the pope or prince into line with the constitution. We have already seen how these concepts influenced Calvin, but he made far less explicit use of them than did his Huguenot successors such as Beza. Like John Knox of Scotland, Beza also made use of the Lutheran Magdeburg Confession, which asserted the duty of the people to depose a ruler who abused the terms of the agreements under which he ruled, particularly when he failed to defend the true religion.[17]

Probably influenced by Calvin's Sermon XXIX on I Samuel 8 (though taking his ideas further), Beza argues when dealing with Samuel's warning to Israel against choosing a king, that although the king would be ordained by God, he should also be elected by the people under specific legal limitation and that he could be deposed for violating these limits.[18] Beza writes:

> There was first an oath by which king and people obligated themselves to God in that they promised to observe His Law both ecclesiastical and political, and then a mutual oath between the king and the people. Then, do the people—that is, the estates of the people—have the right to correct the person they have elevated to dominion, if he does not do his duty? I say they have. . . .[19]

Underlying this "historical" argument was what might be termed a "natural law" or "inherent human rights" concept. Denying the monarchical theory that the people are inherently subservient to their rulers, Beza argues (as Samuel Rutherford did some sixty years later) that "man's fundamental condition must be one of natural liberty"[20] so that instead of "the people being created by the magistrates," the magistrates are "created by the people."[21] On the surface at least, this seems far removed from Saint Paul's teaching of passive obedience in Romans 13, though it does have something in common with Peter's disobedience in Acts 4 as well as with several Old Testament elections and depositions of kings.

Exegetically speaking, Calvin seems to have been closer to a plain reading of Romans 13 than this group of French Huguenot Tractarian followers. Vautier points out that Calvin, like Paul in Romans 13, tended to assume that the existence of the civil magistrate gave it legitimacy as such. And as Pierre Courthial has pointed out, the great majority of Huguenots would have thought like Calvin on Romans 13 rather than like the Tractarians, given their common allegiance to the Reformed confessions (mentioned earlier).[22] Yet as far as the development of Calvinist political thought is concerned, the work of the radical Tractarians is of first-rate importance. Calvin gave little or no attention to tracing the origins of legitimate government to the prior sovereignty of the people. Comparing Calvin to the

Huguenot writer of *Vindiciae Contra Tyrannos* and to Beza on this point, Vautier writes:

> Contrary to Calvin, these two authors take their stand within the field of law. Going beyond the (purely) theological basis for obedience, they seek to ascertain its juridical basis. This point demonstrates the marked difference between their respective positions. For Calvin, the very fact of exercising power is a sufficient title to it, whereas for them, this fact must be undergirded by a prior right which is based in the consent of the people. (My translation.)[23]

Constitutional Arguments for Civil Resistance

At any rate, the idea of the corporate, constitutional rights of the people in the election and deposing of kings with its background in late medieval conciliarism "enabled the Huguenots to insist that their theory of resistance was legal and constitutional in character, and not a mere call to the many-headed multitude to rise up in rebellion against their lawful overlords."[24] It gave them more hope of appeal to moderate Catholics in France, by producing "a wider and less sectarian appeal than the theories developed by the earlier generation of Calvinist arguments."[25]

Beza's ideas were developed—with new additions—in the last major Huguenot tract we consider, *Vindiciae Contra Tyrannos* (1579). It was probably written by the Huguenot theologian Du Plessis-Mornay (1549-1623) or perhaps by (or in collaboration with) Hubert Languet.[26] For the sake of convenience, we shall call the author of *Vindicae* by his pen-name, "Brutus." Like Beza, Brutus is strongly dependent on radical Catholic conciliarist thought. Skinner explains:

> When he turns to the question of tyranny in the *Defence* [scil. *Vindiciae*], he explicitly refers us to Aquinas, Bartolus, Baldus, and the codifiers of the Roman law. And when he considers the central question of the right to resist, he reveals a close dependence on the radical background of conciliarist thought. He quotes several decisions made at Constance and Basle, refers us on two occasions specifically to the "Sorbonnists," and employs the theories of Gerson,

> Almain, and Mair [scil. Major] in order to defend the idea of an exact analogy between the thesis of conciliarism in the Church and of popular sovereignty in the commonwealth.[27]

Brutus makes less reference than Hotman and Beza to the French Estates, for "by 1574-1575, the Huguenots confronted an organized and widespread movement of Catholic militants opposed to toleration and could no longer count upon support from the Estates. . . ."[28] Hence, Brutus laid more emphasis on the magistrates than on the Estates. The magistrates, he held, represented the whole people (where the true power lay) and were obligated to guard their rights. According to his analysis of both European and biblical history:

> . . . officers of the kingdom whom the people have established, or the majority of these, or any one of them, very gravely sin against the Covenant with God if they do not use force against a king who corrupts God's Law or prevents its restoration, in order to confine him to his proper bounds. . . .
>
> For as the entire people is above the king, so these officers, although below the king as individuals, are above him when taken as a body. . . .[29]

The underlying theory is a species of covenantal thought: the bilateral contract.[30] The first part of the contract is between God and the king, by which the king is ordained to rule justly in accordance with God's law (discussed in the first *Quaestio* of *Vindiciae*). The second part of the contract (discussed in the second *Quaestio*) is the covenant between God and the people, to insure that the commonwealth is ruled in accordance with divine law.

If the king fails in his duty to uphold the law, the lesser magistrates have the right "to use force against a king."[31] As Vautier points out, the bilateral contract is a way of asserting that even in appointing a king, the people always retain their original sovereignty by means of specifically imposed conditions.[32] Thus, Brutus shows that the major end of civil government must always be "to protect the people's liberty and safety."[33]

Any king who does not care for the people's welfare, but "persistently subverts the commonwealth . . . brazenly perverts the law . . .

[and] shows that pledges, covenants, justice, and religion mean nothing to him . . ." is labeled by Brutus "a tyrant"—"an enemy of God and man."[34]

Brutus then refers to Bartolus, who taught that the king could be deposed by his superior. "But the superior here is the whole people or those who represent the people. . . . they may call the people to arms."[35] His reasoning is close to that of John Knox's *Appellation to the Nobility of Scotland* (1554), but does not go quite so far as Knox's 1558 *Letter to the Commonalty*, which grants the common people the right and duty of revolution if their leaders refuse to act to protect the true religion. However, Brutus's argumentation is less explicitly religious than that of Knox (not concentrating, as does Knox, on the scriptural duty to put down idolatry), again presumably because of the need to appeal to the moderate Catholic population in France.

Change from Covenant to Constitution

This Huguenot change of emphasis from strictly religious and covenantal to more generally political and constitutional theory marked a new epoch in Calvinist church-state discussions. Skinner summarized this change:

> . . . with Beza, Mornay [scil. Brutus] and their followers, the idea that the preservation of religious uniformity constitutes the sole possible grounds for legitimate resistance is finally abandoned. The result is a fully *political* theory of revolution, founded on a recognisably modern, secularized thesis about the natural rights and original sovereignty of the people.[36]

Vindiciae is forward-looking in another significant respect. By its emphasis on the subordination of the prince to a rule of law, expressed through a Parliament representing the people, it anticipates the later Scottish Presbyterian concept of separation of powers in order, as Vautier expresses it, "To prevent the excesses of power" (my translation).[37] Later, from a very different perspective, Montesquieu and Rousseau would discuss in more detail this same question. But in the 1570s, such explicit discussion as was found in Brutus was "extremely rare at that time" (my translation).[38]

International Influence of Huguenot Thought

Calvinists were a minority in France, they failed militarily, and their religious and political constitutional arguments did not prevail in France at that time.

> Despite this political failure, the constitutionalism of this period had a permanent effect on the development of political thought. The ideas that the king was subject to the people or their representatives and that representative bodies were properly supreme are not a mere anticipation of doctrine later to be developed independently, but the source of a continuing tradition.[39]

The Dutch Rebellion against the Spanish in 1580 drew inspiration from the Huguenot writers,[40] as did English constitutional theorists of the seventeenth century.[41] Roman Catholic scholars such as the Jesuit Mariana[42] and French Holy League polemicist Jean Boucher (1548-1644)[43] adapted Huguenot "monarchomach" arguments for their own purposes (as the Calvinists had earlier adapted Catholic radical conciliarism). They were concerned over the prospect of Protestant Henry of Navarre becoming direct heir to the throne of France in 1584 after the death of the Duke of Anjou.

Vautier appears to be correct in assessing the influence of the Huguenot monarchomachs on the eighteenth-century French Enlightenment as a relatively small one:

> In retrospect, the Huguenots were one of the currents from which the Natural Law School drew. These Tractarians built the bridge between the doctrines of the Reformers and those of this [later] "Protestant School," which manifested a strongly rationalistic tendency. (My translation.)[44]

Yet their influence in the generally less "rationalist" and more Protestant-oriented American colonies seems to have been larger than in prerevolutionary France. John Adams mentioned *Vindiciae* as important for understanding American independence and the Constitution.[45]

Perhaps more than anywhere else, however, several of the major concepts of the French Huguenots found time and environment to develop in Scotland, where fellow Calvinists already shared a common stock of theology and ideas well before the monarchomachs published their tracts.

Vautier summarizes the enduring Huguenot monarchomach concepts as: the limited character of power, sovereignty of the people, and the right to resist tyrants in the name of divinely granted liberty.[46] We shall now proceed to view how historical circumstances made Scotland a fruitful field for the systematic cultivation and growth of these (and other) aspects of the Calvinist religious and political heritage.

Notes

[1] See his *Declaration* in *Memoires de Conde*. 6 vols (London: La Haye, 1743), 3:222-35.

[2] Calvin, C. O. 17:396-97.

[3] In a personal communication to me (3 September 1988) Monsieur Pierre Courthial, honorary dean of the Faculty of Reformed Theology at Aix-en-Provence, stated:

> After 1567, the Huguenots remained as anti-revolutionary and royalist as previously. One must pray, sigh, wait, hope. The only authentic republican of the sixteenth century in France was La Boetie, the friend of Montaigne. But he was Roman Catholic.
>
> When a Protestant confederation was formed at Millau in l'Aveyran in 1573, under the presidency of Jacques de Castelpers, the entire delegation from France swore an oath of fidelity to the Crown, "having no other goal than the glory of God, the advancement of the Kingdom of Christ, the maintenance and service of this Crown, and the general welfare of this kingdom." In line with the Reformed doctrine of the responsibility of lesser magistrates in time of crisis among superior magistrates, they thus designated the Prince Henri de Bourbon, "Lieutenant-General of His Majesty" as heir of the Crown.

[4] Pierre Courthial, "The Golden Age of Calvinism in France, 1533-1633" in *John Calvin: His Influence in the Western World*, ed. W. S. Reid (Grand Rapids: Zondervan, 1982), p. 79.

[5] Quentin Skinner, *The Foundations of Modern Political Thought* (Cambridge: Cambridge University Press, 1978), 2:310.

[6] Julian H. Franklin, ed. *Constitutionalism and Resistance in the Sixteenth Century: Three Treatises by Hotman, Beza and Mornay* (New York: Pegasus, 1969), p. 19.

[7] Ibid., p. 20.

[8] Ibid., p. 21.

[9] Ibid.

[10] Ibid., p. 25.

[11] Skinner, *Foundations*, p. 313.

[12] Ibid., p. 318.

[13] Ibid., p. 319.

[14] Ibid.

[15] Franklin, *Constitutionalism and Resistance*, p. 30.

[16] Skinner, *Foundations*, p. 320; cf. Franklin, *Constitutionalism and Resistance*, pp. 30, 37, 38.

[17] Franklin, *Constitutionalism and Resistance*, pp. 31, 32.

[18] Ibid., p.38.

[19] Ibid., p. 118.

[20] Skinner, *Foundations*, p. 326.

[21] Beza, *Right of Magistrates*, in Franklin, ed., *Constitutionalism and Resistance*, p. 104. See for instance such coronations and depositions of kings by the people as in Judges 8:22; 9:6; II Samuel 16:18; I Kings 16; II Kings 10; 14:21; etc. Such passages would later be cited by the Scots theologian, Samuel Rutherford, in *Lex, Rex*, as a justification for overturning an oppressive monarchy (see his discussion of these passages in "Question IV").

[22] Courthial adds, "*Vindiciae Contra Tyrannos* was written by Hubert Languet (1518-1581) and is not the work of a faithful Huguenot, but of a denationalized French Protestant, who had the impudence to return to the court of France as an ambassador of the German princes!" (personal communication of 3 September 1988).

[23] "Au contraire de Calvin, ces deux auteurs se placent sur le terrain du droit; en plus du fondement theologique de l'obeissance, ils recherchent son fondement juridique. Sur ce point se marque nettement la difference de leurs positions respectives. Pour Calvin, le fait meme d'exercer le pouvoir est un titre suffisant, alors que pour eux ce fait doit se doubler d'un droit, qui nait du consentement du peuple." Vautier, *Les Theories*, p. 120. See also pp. 122, 127, 130.

[24] Skinner, *Foundations*, p. 334.

[25] Ibid., p. 335.

[26] See discussion of authorship in Vautier, *Les Theories*, pp. 15-29.

[27] Skinner, *Foundations*, p. 321.

[28] Franklin, *Constitutionalism and Resistance*, p. 40.

[29] Ibid., p. 162.

[30] Old Testament scholars with expert knowledge in ancient Near Eastern covenant formulations have distinguished two basic types of ancient Near Eastern covenants and treaties: unilateral (with all conditions laid down by the superior authority) and bilateral (with conditions mutually agreed upon between equals). God's covenant with Abraham in Genesis 15 is an example of the former, and David and Jonathan's covenant with each other in Samuel is an example of the latter. See

Mendenhall, *Law and Covenant in Israel and the Ancient Near East* (Pittsburgh: The Presbyterian Board of Colportage of Western Pennsylvania, 1955).

[31] Franklin, *Constitutionalism and Resistance*, p. 157.

[32] Vautier, *Les Theories*, p. 100.

[33] Franklin, *Constitutionalism and Resistance*, p. 168.

[34] Ibid., p. 190.

[35] Ibid., p. 191.

[36] Skinner, *Foundations*, p. 338.

[37] "D'empecher les exces du pouvoir." Vautier, *Les Theories*, p. 147.

[38] "Fort rare a l'epoque." Ibid.

[39] Franklin, *Constitutionalism and Resistance*, p. 45.

[40] Ibid., pp. 45, 139; Skinner, *Foundations*, pp. 337, 338. Also, Robert M. Kingdon, "The Political Resistance of the Calvinists in France and the Low Countries During the Sixteenth Century," *The Journal of Modern History* 27, 3 (1958): 220-33.

[41] See J. H. M. Salmon, *The French Religious Wars in European Political Thought* (Oxford: Oxford University Press, 1959).

[42] According to Franklin, *Constitutionalism and Resistance*, p. 205 n. 74, "The influence on Jesuit theorists of the sixteenth century like Mariana is indirect and is filtered through the League." See Guenter Lewy, *Constitutionalism and Statecraft in the Golden Age of Spain: A Study of the Political Thought of Juan de Mariana* (Geneva: DVOC, 1960), Travaux d'Humanisme et Renaissance, XXXVI.

[43] See Vautier, *Les Theories*, p. 158, and Skinner, *Foundations*, pp. 345, 348.

[44] "Ils [the Huguenots] furent, en revanche, l'un des courants ou puisa l'ecole du Droit naturel, ils firent le pont entre les doctrines des reformateurs et celles de cette 'ecole protestante,' ou se manifeste deja fortement la tendance rationaliste." Vautier, *Les Theories*, p. 161.

[45] John Adams, *Works* (Boston: Charles C. Little and James Brown, 1851), 6:4.

[46] Vautier, *Les Theories*, pp. 164, 165.

3

Calvinism in Scotland: Controversy and Triumph

IMBART DE LA TOUR has spoken of Calvin's legacy as consisting of a book, the *Institutes of the Christian Religion*, and also of a city, Geneva.[1] It served as a model for Reformers elsewhere, none more so than the great Scots Reformer, John Knox, who called it "the most perfect school of Christ since the days of the Apostles."[2] But if Geneva was in many, though never all, respects an example of Calvinism in a city-state, Knox's Scotland exemplified it perhaps more fully than anywhere else in the world on a national level. Calvin's teaching on God, authority, law, and church and state developed further in Scotland than it could in France (owing to the minority position of the Huguenots) or in England (owing to the predominance of other theories of church-state relations).

While Knox owed much to Calvin for his understanding of theology and of the foundational authority of Scripture over all of life, he disagreed with his mentor on important points such as resistance to the civil magistrate. He was also more influenced by the Old Testament theocracy, and rather less by natural law, than Calvin. Thus the Scottish Reformation both developed implicit teachings of Calvin on a national scene and went beyond them in a more radical direction. This direction later proved in part to be "the wave of the future."

Three Concepts of Post-Reformation Scottish Government

The peculiar approach of Reformed Scotland to God, church, and civil government was a major stage in the development of modern political systems in the West. Three concepts especially were realized in Scottish government: the concept of the church as a body equal in legal right and standing with the civil state; the implicitly "covenantal" idea of the direct rights of the people to hold political authorities responsible to carry out their functions under limitations prescribed by transcendent law; and the general elevation of the common citizen through democratizing structures emulating Presbyterian polity. It would, however, take nearly a century and a half from the peak of Knox's influence on Scotland in the 1560s until these principles were worked out and established in British parliamentary function in various actions from 1690 to 1707.

The Reformation came fairly late to Scotland, which in the Reformation era was in an almost continually turbulent situation. This was due in part to a weak central state with jealous rivalries between monarchs (who were often children represented by powerful regents) and an unruly feudal nobility. National stability was also undermined by a rather corrupt set of Roman Catholic prelates such as Cardinal David Beaton, political "strong man" of the kingdom and father of several illegitimate children. He was assassinated by Reformed associates of Knox at St. Andrews in 1546. Scotland with its weak central government became a pawn between Protestant England and Catholic France, whose boy king, Francis II was married to Scotland's girl queen, Mary Stuart. This international rivalry assumed particularly direct influence on the shape of the Reformation in Scotland after the accession of Elizabeth I in England in 1558 and after the death of Francis II in France in 1560.

The earliest impulses to reform in Scotland had been Lutheran, but Calvinism came increasingly to the fore with the Reformer George Wishart (1512-46), who had been exiled in Europe and there influenced by thinkers such as Bucer, Bullinger, and especially Calvin.[3] Shortly before Wishart's martyrdom by the Catholic authorities, John Knox came under his influence and was converted to Protestantism. Soon Knox was captured, made a slave on a French galley ship, and eventually, through the good offices of important officials in the English government, released. Knox rapidly rose to prominence in the English court and was a chaplain to the pro-Calvinist boy king, Edward VI (died 1553). Along with many other Protestant English church leaders, Knox fled to the continent upon the accession of Mary Tudor, who outlawed Protestantism and attempted to reimpose Roman Catholicism by force.

John Knox and other English church statesmen (such as Goodman, Ponet, and Foxe) eventually took refuge in Calvin's Geneva, where Knox became pastor of the English-speaking church of the refugees. During Knox's absence from Scotland, he kept closely in touch with religious and political events transpiring at home in hopes of eventual return. This return was to become a reality soon after the death of Mary Tudor in 1558, owing particularly to the activity of the Scottish "Lords of the Congregation" in the late 1550s.

Scottish Development of the Covenant Concept

These members of the aristocracy who were proreform, were in competition with the regent, Mary of Guise, mother of Mary Stuart, who as a convinced Roman Catholic was working against reform and for an alliance with her native France. John Knox, at risk to his life, spent some six months in 1555 encouraging the efforts of "the Lords" to take the Reformation to the population, extirpate the Mass, and take over the civil government. Through Knox's teaching, and in the favorable climate of Scotland's religious, political, intellectual heritage, much of the theoretical justification for the fight these "Lords of the Congregation" waged against Mary of Guise was based on the concept of covenant. Covenant was to be a lasting theme in the Scottish Reformation and its aftermath, one in which they would go far beyond Calvin. In so doing, they would leave a legacy to be selectively appropriated by later generations, though those who followed were not committed to the theological context in which these concepts took shape.

Shortly after his forced exile in 1554, Knox wrote *An Admonition or Warning That the Faithful Christians in London, etc. . . . May Avoid God's Vengeance.* His central idea was that believers must covenant (or "be in league") "betwixt God and us, that He alone shall be our God and we shall be His people . . . we shall seek to Him and we shall flee from all strange gods." This meant opposing idolatry in order to remain in covenant with the true God and thus avoid eternal damnation.[4] Knox dealt with covenant again in a tract on baptism in 1556,[5] but stated his views most fully in his 1558 *Appellation* to the nobility, estates, and commonwealth of Scotland. Here Knox based his concept of a covenant that binds government and people under the law of God very firmly on his understanding of the Old Testament. He cited King Josiah's calling the Israelites to obey the rediscovered law (II Kings 23). Hence temporal rulers must reform religion and extirpate idolatry. Obviously Knox thought one could go directly from the Old Testament to his own times, though others such as George Buchanan would question the validity of transferring the practices of a Judaic theocracy onto a modern European kingdom. But assuming as Knox did a direct correspondence between several (selectively chosen) aspects of Old Testament civil law and that of a modern Christian kingdom, Knox quite naturally called for action on the basis of such Old Testament examples as King Asa's covenant with his people to serve the true God (II Chron. 15).

Knox Goes Beyond Calvin

Knox went even further in his late 1558 *Letter to the Commonalty of Scotland*, which was written after his disappointment that the Reformed nobility were not taking sufficient action. Here he goes utterly beyond Calvin (and anticipates some elements of the 1570s French Huguenot thinking of civil resistance) and advocates the duty of the common people to see that Christ is truly preached and idolatry overthrown in case the nobles and estates refused. Basing his argument on various biblical texts (especially Exod. 34) that teach a covenant between God and his people (not just their leaders), Knox argues that to refuse to resist an idolatrous regime is to run the risk of losing one's immortal soul.

Knox's emphasis on covenant met a receptive hearing with "the Lords of the Congregation," due in part to their Scottish background of traditionally engaging in various civil and religious "bands," rooted in Scots medieval feudalism.[6] Their receptivity was due also to what A. H. Williamson (in *Scottish National Consciousness in the Age of James VI*) refers to as a Scottish participation in the general British Protestant apocalypticism of the sixteenth century, though with a different "twist."

There was a general view held by frequently persecuted British Reformers that they were living in the last age when "Antichrist" (to many of them, Roman Catholicism or the pope) would be overthrown and a new reign of righteousness inaugurated with universal political-religious changes. According to Williamson, the English Reformers, such as Knox's friend during Geneva exile, John Foxe, author of Foxe's *Book of Martyrs*, had a long, documented religious and legal history which gave them their identity as the elect people of God. However, the Scots, being on the losing side of many wars and invasions that had destroyed a high percentage of their records, had no such impressive written legal and religious history to give them this desired identity. Hence, Williamson argues that they were peculiarly open to the concept and practice of covenanting, which—in a different way from Foxe's recital of historic English martyrdoms or Coke's glorification of the liberating precedents of ancient English common law—provided an identity as an elect people in terms of present and future relationships with God.

Referring particularly to the covenanting that occurred in Scotland in the 1630s, long after Knox's time, Williamson writes:

> Englishmen appealed to law; Scotsmen appealed to the instrument which determined the law [scil. the covenant]. Scotland had never had an "ancient constitution" in the English sense. Her public culture required a dynamism distinctly its own while responding to this circumstance.[7]

Essentially, the Lords of the Congregation were an alternative, revolutionary government. Encouraged by Knox's writings to act against the queen regent's noncovenantal government (which they considered idolatrous because of its support of Roman Catholic images and the Mass), they won a preliminary victory in 1560, owing to Elizabeth I's fear of Catholic France's using Scotland as a route for invasion of England. After the opening of hostilities between the forces of the Lords of the Congregation and those of the queen regent (following a riot in Perth in 1559), Elizabeth intervened to support the Reformed Lords.[8] The queen regent died in 1560 and the French troops withdrew. The Scottish Parliament met in 1560 with Knox on hand to give guidance in the work of covenanted Reformation.

At this point we can see the historic importance of Knox's more radical Hebraic view of the covenant, compared with that of Calvin. Knox parted company with Calvin, and also with John Major (who had taught Knox as well as Calvin and Buchanan),[9] when he held that God's covenant with the people gave them the direct right to rebel against ungodly magistrates, whether or not "lesser magistrates" gave them guidance.

As Greaves summarizes:

> Before Knox left Geneva he had transposed the religious covenant or league freely and smoothly into the political realm, where it became allied with the traditional Scottish band and the natural law-social contract theory, which was of major significance in British and American political history in the following centuries. The ultimate divergence of Knox and Calvin on the nature of lawful rebellion against temporal sovereigns can be traced to their different interpretations of the covenant. It was Knox, not Calvin, who was willing to contend for the right of the people actively to resist a tyrannical monarch. The covenant was an idea with awesome political potency, as Knox demonstrated, and as the French Huguenots and the English Puritans as well as Knox's Scottish followers subsequently discovered.[10]

Legal Consolidation of Scottish Reformation

Under the leadership of the victorious Lords of the Congregation, Parliament met in August, 1560. "By the Papal Jurisdiction Act

1560 c. 2, it abolished the jurisdiction of the Pope in Scotland. Further the Act 1560 c. 3 abolished idolatry, and c. 4 proscribed the Mass."[11] The Parliament set up a committee under John Knox to prepare a new statement of Reformed belief. Completed in four days and clearly Calvinist in inspiration, it was called "the Scots Confession." Based on the biblical history of redemption from Adam to Christ to the church, it makes a classically Protestant statement on how the true church can be discerned (i.e., the "marks" or "notes" of the church):

> The notes, signes and assured tokens whereby the immaculate spouse of Christ Jesus is knawen fra the horrible harlot, the Kirk malignent, we affirme, are nouther Antiquitie, Title, usurpit lineal Descence, Place appointed, nor multitude of men approving ane error . . . [but are] . . . the trew preaching of the Words of God . . . the right administration of the sacraments . . . ecclesiastical discipline.[12]

Adopted by Parliament in the Confession of Faith Act of 1560 c. 1., it was said to be

> the Confession of Faith professed and believed by the Protestants within the realm of Scotland, published by them in Scotland, and by the Estates thereof ratified and approved as wholesome and sound doctrine, grounded upon the infallible truth of God's Word.

Professor Frank Lyall suggests careful attention to the precise implications of these words of adoption:

> The Confession does not bear to be enacted by the civil authority for the Church. It is the Confession published by the Protestants in Scotland, and *ratified and approved* by Parliament. The civil authority does not act, it approves a statement formulated outside of itself. Again, the Confession is not the Confession of the Church of Scotland at this stage. Nor is it adopted or put forward by authority of that Church. It is the Confession of the Protestants in Scotland, and no institutional church is referred to.[13]

John Knox's committee was also ordered to draw up a constitution for the church, which they did as *The First Book of Discipline*.[14] Presented to Parliament in 1560 and again in 1561, it was rejected because of the financial requirements of its proposals. It formulated

> a system of church government, based on a modified episcopal concept. It envisaged a Christian commonwealth in which the Church and the State would cooperate, the Church being responsible for the welfare of the people, while the civil authority would govern. The Church would deal with all such matters as education, and poor relief in addition to its more obvious functions of preaching and discipline.[15]

The scheme was unacceptable to the Lords because it proposed that the endowment of the Roman Catholic Church be given to support these functions of the church. Some of the Lords had already taken over church properties, and others received income from ecclesiastical estates. Thus economic self-interest dampened reforming zeal.

"Higher Authorities" and the Highest Authority

Hence the Scots reforming ministers both won and lost political contests. But continuing religious-political skirmishes between Protestants and Catholics, and between various factions of the Protestants as well, should be understood in light of the Reformers' view of ultimate authority. All Protestants were united in claiming to be under the direct authority of God speaking in Holy Scripture, rather than under the authority of the Vatican and its hierarchy and tradition. Knox and his Scottish colleagues were no different on this foundational doctrine, except that they took it further than Luther and Calvin (as did later the Puritans in England).

The First Book of Discipline defined idolatry as "all honouring of God not contained in his Holy Word."[16] Hence they, parting company with the more liturgical Lutherans and with many of the Anglicans and some continental Reformed, excluded among other traditional Christian practices "holy days" (such as Christmas), "because in God's Scripture they neither have commandment nor assurance."[17] As Cameron points out, this meant that in 1566 when the Scottish Church was asked to approve the Swiss Calvinist Second Helvetic

Confession, they did so only with the exception of the passage "concerning the festival of our Lord's nativity, circumcision, passion, resurrection, ascension and sending the Holy Ghost upon his disciples." [18]

In a notable phrase, The Scots Confession submitted itself to the authority of Scripture to such a degree that its six writers requested to be notified if anything should be found in it out of accord with Scripture.[19] In a 1554 letter to the Christians of London, New Castle, and Berwick, Knox wrote of "the very simplicity and plain infallible truth of God's Word."[20] He attacked the Mass on the authority of "the infallible Word of God" revealed in the "whole body of God's Scriptures."[21]

As Greaves explains:

> Unlike Luther, Knox conceived of the unity of Scripture in such fashion that the rigor of Old Testament precepts was not ordinarily mitigated by the subjection of the Old Testament to the New. Knox did not stress discontinuity or supersedure in the Scriptures, but like Calvin, freely employed passages from various parts of the Bible, whether Old or New, to confirm one another. . . . The applicability of the Old Testament to contemporary concerns is particularly evident in Knox's views on political matters, notably gynecocracy.[22]

An understanding of Knox's view of the authority of all of God's Word, as he saw it, gives insight into his conduct with Mary, Queen of Scots. In this light, it is missing the point to focus on the harsh nature of Knox's interviews with his queen. He was sensitive to this charge and specifically explained his position:

> When thai sall teiche me, be Godis plaine written word, that the repruife of vice is a civile and prophane thing, and that it is a thing that perteaneth not to the ministrie, I sall do as Godis word commandis me: Bot vnot' that tyme . . . I mon that sentence and power pronounced and gevin be God to his prophetis, be Jeremie and Ezechiell, to stand for a perpetuall law and rewle to all true ministers. . . .[23]

Therefore Knox, as a man under higher authority, had no alternative but to argue with Mary Stuart. She had come across from France in 1560 as a young widow to begin her reign over Scotland.

Holding definite Catholic convictions, she wished to stop the reform movement in order to reestablish traditional Catholicism (or "idolatry" in Knox's strongly Protestant view).

In his fourth and final interview with the queen, she asked him what standing he had to attack her proposed Spanish marriage. His answer indicates how, to his mind, the higher authority of God's Word made it right for a person of the lower ranks to rebuke a magistrate of the highest standing in terms of the supreme divine authority:

> What have you to do with my marriage? Or what are you within this Commonwealth?
>
> A subject, Madam, born within the same. And albeit I neither be Earl, Lord nor Baron within it, yet has God made me (how abject that ever I be in your eyes) a profitable member within the same: Yea, Madam, to me it pertains no less to forewarn of such things as may hurt it, if I foresee them, than it does to any of the Nobility.[24]

Knox and the Old Testament

From this conviction, one can see that though the Calvinist Reformers never set out to be levellers in society (and indeed spoke against it), yet their views on higher authority could, depending on the circumstances, lead in that direction. Resistance to "idolatrous" authorities thus followed as a way of necessary obedience to the highest authority: God speaking in Scripture. Knox was clearly influenced in his reasoning by the Lutheran Magdeburg Confession of 1550, which he quotes in his *Works* (as he relates the substance of a Catholic-Protestant debate).[25] He was also influenced by the English Marian exiles of Geneva such as Ponet and Goodman, or we may say that the influence was mutual.[26] But by far the greatest source of Knox's thought on resistance was the Scriptures, especially the Old Testament. Knox had written two tracts, one in 1554 and another in 1558,[27] showing, in his view, that the "historical context was . . . not unlike that in which the Hebrew prophets had been commanded to speak the divine Word."[28] God's Word "took precedence over material gains, personal relationships, and even civil laws."[29]

As Greaves writes:

> . . . the Old Testament provided ample examples of the deposition of rulers. Following biblical precepts as he understood them, he extended the right of rebellion against idolatrous and tyrannical sovereigns from the magistrates and nobility to the elect. . . . Beza and later Huguenot writers were among those influenced, as perhaps was Calvin.[30]

The theocentric, Old Testament covenantal structure of Knox's thought, which required direct revolution by the people against an unscriptural regime as a religious duty entering into the eternal well-being of one's soul, had a different atmosphere from *De Jure Regni Apud Scotos*[31] by the famous classical humanist scholar and (after his conversion to Calvinism) revolutionary thinker, George Buchanan. Buchanan, a native Scot, taught both Montaigne in Bordeaux and the young James VI in Stirling Castle. Buchanan based the right of the people to revolution not directly on a religious covenant, but on an inherent popular right of "the whole body of the people" to elect a ruler without alienating their original sovereignty, which still gives them the right to depose him, if necessary.[32] Buchanan followed Knox in granting the whole people the right of revolution, but differed in making it more of a natural political right than a scriptural, covenantally defined religious duty.

A New Concept of "Political Rights"

Althusius of Westphalia in Germany (1557-1638), another influential Calvinist political theorist of the next generation, followed Buchanan in ignoring discussion of the covenant in order to provide a more purely political concentration on "the conception of rights, not religious duties"[33] in his 1603 *Politics Methodically Set Forth.* Althusius was in Buchanan's line, for unlike Knox's Hebraic emphasis, Buchanan held that "because of its unique, sacred character, Israel was irrelevant to other societies which could only be legitimately founded upon popular sovereignty."[34]

As we shall see in following chapters, Knox's emphasis on religious covenant would be basic to the opening phase of the English Revolution involving the Puritan struggle in the 1630s and 1640s, whereas Buchanan's and Althusius's political rights emphasis (as filtered through others) would be basic to the closing phase of the English Revolution, the 1688 "Glorious Revolution," as well as one strand in the tangled skein leading to the American Revolution of 1776.

It is an interesting question as to whether the later "political rights" theory could have come into prominence had the way not been prepared for it by the religious covenant concept of Knox, who advanced beyond Calvin's reserve in order to do so. It is doubtful that talk of "political rights" would have sufficiently motivated the masses of mid-sixteenth-century Scotland, whose frame of reference was fundamentally a Christian one, to take possibly life-threatening action. Political and economic expediency, class conflict, and international intrigue no doubt had a strong role to play. Yet it seems to have been Knox's ability to articulate religious concerns (particularly the gain or loss of eternal salvation) in a way directly related to political action that exercised such a broad appeal. Both rulers and ruled among the population were finally won for Calvinism in Scotland.

From this point of view, Knox is a stage on the road from Calvin to Buchanan and Althusius. Knox radicalized the resistance concepts of Calvin, and popularized them on a national scale. Buchanan, Althusius, and later political theorists could then take the Knoxian theological concept of covenantally based popular resistance, and broaden its appeal to a wider population by removing it from its explicitly theological context.

Continuing Church-State Struggles in Scotland

Knox and the Reformation in Scotland affected later legal and political theory and practice in much of the Western world in more ways than justifying popular resistance to a tyrannical civil order. Of at least equal importance was the working out of a theory of ongoing church and state relations, which was to have important implications for related political and legal matters, such as the plurality of civil governmental jurisdictions and powers, as well as the coordination and limitation of governmental powers based on objective and transcendent standards. Yet it was to take well over a century of struggle after the time of Knox for these concepts of limited and representative powers to be substantially established. And indeed, for nearly two more centuries after the 1690 settlement, the church-state balance in Scotland was to suffer occasional upsets.

Queen Mary Stuart was forced to abdicate in 1567, which meant that the Catholic monarch was replaced by her infant son, James VI, on whose behalf the Protestant Earl of Moray acted as regent. The Parliament of 1567 again repealed support of the papacy and reestablished the Scots Confession. The Scottish Parliament then proceeded to establish the Reformed Church. The Church Act of 1567 c. 6 (reenacted with fuller explanation in 1579 as c. 6) stated:

> Our sovereign Lord with advice of his three estates . . . has declared and declares. . . . And the people of this realme that professis Jesus christ as he is now offerit in his evangell and do communicat with the haly sacramentis as in the reformit kirkis of this realme at publictlie administrat according to the confession of the fayth To be the only trew and haly kirk of Jesus Christ within this realme.[35]

Thus the Reformed Church was the only one recognized by law in Scotland. Then the jurisdiction of this church was dealt with in Church Jurisdiction Act 1567 c.12, which declares that the crown

> declarit and grantit iurisdictioun to the said Kirk quhilk [which] consistis and standis in preicheing of the trew word of Jesus Christ correctioun of maneris and administratioun of haly Sacramentis . . . thair is na uther face of Kirk nor uther face of Religion than is presentlie be the Savour of God establischeit within this Realme.[36]

Frank Lyall raises a difficult point of interpretation:

> The terms of this Act do not make it clear whether the State was recognizing that jurisdiction which the church had undoubtedly

> been exercising from 1560, or whether the "grant" additional to the declaration involved a conferral of power by the State. It was interpreted in the latter form in the Disruption cases [scil. in the 1843 split of the Church of Scotland over state interference in the election of pastors owing to "lay patronage"], conforming to the then prevalent legal theory, but this may have been wrong. . . . That ambiguity was to be productive of much strife in the future.[37]

The Church of Scotland: Presbyterian or Episcopalian?

Interestingly and surprisingly, these legal statutes did not specify the particular type of polity to prevail in the Church of Scotland. "In fact for the next twenty-five years the church was without a defined polity, and moved from quasi-episcopacy to quasi-presbyterianism and back, depending upon a variety of factors."[38] The ultimate victory of Presbyterian polity over Episcopalian was due in considerable measure to Knox's influential successor, Andrew Melville, who returned home from Geneva in 1574. He was both a Reformed minister and a university academic, very concerned with the reform of schools and universities.[39] When Melville returned to Scotland to take up church leadership, "he found that the episcopal system then in force was being used by the Crown to control the church, and by the nobility to continue to divert church funds into their coffers."[40] Whether rightly or wrongly, Melville perceived the office of bishop as such to be the root of the problem and thus was determined to replace Episcopacy with full-fledged Presbyterianism (which was already operating on a national scale among the Huguenots in France).

As Knox differed in important respects from Calvin, so Melville differed in some significant areas from Knox. Gordon Donaldson has impressively argued that neither Calvin nor Knox was necessarily opposed to the function of bishops in and of itself,[41] although both were opposed to the theory of apostolic succession of the power of the keys through Episcopal ordination. But Melville went beyond both in theologically opposing the very existence of government by bishops (even apart from theories of apostolic succession) on the basis of his reading of biblical polity. He spoke for Presbyterian government by representative elders ruling in a series of graded courts, from local church session to regional synod to national general assembly, with powers of review, control, and jurisdictional appeal. This would uphold the headship of Christ and the legitimate liberties of the people. In his view, the rule of bishops derogated the sole authority of Christ and was detrimental to the liberties of the people. Obviously not all Reformed thinkers, then or since, have agreed with him on this matter. (The Reformed Church in Hungary has had bishops for centuries). Yet undoubtedly Melville did have a point in noticing how the king at that time was using his bishops to weaken the ability of the Reformed churches to exercise their functions freely within their own jurisdiction.

In addition to the entanglement of church polity with the king and with those of his bishops who were seeking greater control, there was a further entanglement of church polity with economic struggles. The general assembly of the Scottish Church wanted the property and wealth of the ancient Catholic Church for support of the ministry, education of the people, and assistance to the poor. But the Parliament who represented to a large degree the land-owning class, were benefiting from the unsettled estate of "the patrimonie of the Kirk." Maintaining ancient bishoprics was often seen by them as a way of keeping the church's wealth for the ruling classes and crown, rather than using it for the needs of the Reformed ministry and the people.[42]

To deal with the entangled problem of state intrusion into affairs of the Reformed church, Melville drew up *The Second Book of Discipline*, which was adopted by the general assembly in 1578.

The Second Book condemned Episcopacy for its possible abuse and set out clearly and cogently the Presbyterian doctrine of conciliar church government. *The Second Book* stated, rather than argued, the independency of the church from civil authority, church powers and authority being derived from God.[43]

This last point was to be of highest importance in clarifying and systematizing the Scottish Calvinist view of church-state relations, which in the future would in turn be widely influential throughout much of Western society. Since Christ, in accordance with the New Testament, is head of his church and rules it directly by his Word and Spirit:

> the church was not deemed to have received its jurisdiction from God intermediately through the prince, as was claimed in England where the Henrician act for the restraint of appeals had declared that all jurisdictions, spiritual and temporal, were derived from the crown. ... Instead *The [Second] Book* postulated the existence of two parallel, divinely ordained jurisdictions, separate and distinct, yet co-ordinate. The phraseology of the "two kingdoms" was not employed to describe the relationship, but the implication was there. . . . Any notion of intermediate, earthly headship of the church, either papal or princely, was positively denounced. . . .[44]

The "Two-Kingdoms" Concept of Presbyterians

The strength of the Presbyterian party with its "two-kingdoms" view postulating the immediate headship of Christ over the church, increased in influence, so that the Scottish Parliament re-established Presbyterian polity in 1579. However, King James VI worked hard to maintain as much control as possible over the Presbyterian church. In 1584 Parliament passed "the Black Acts," which attempted to reimpose Episcopacy and place ecclesiastical affairs under the crown. But again, the Presbyterians regained strength so that their polity was reestablished in 1592 in an act of Parliament traditionally known as "the Great Charter of the Church."

Many of the religious-political struggles of the next hundred years were based on this question of who is head of the church. This pivotal question played a significant part in the civil wars of the English Revolution in its various phases from the 1640s to the 1680s. (In his theological history of Scottish Calvinism, James Walker devoted a chapter to it.)[45] But the struggle started well before the mid-seventeenth century. James VI definitely preferred Erastianism, the theory that the state has final control over the church. Hence Andrew Melville articulated the deepest concerns of Scottish Presbyterianism when, in a famous interview with James in Falkland Palace in 1596, he pulled the sleeve of the king and called him "God's sillie vassal," reminding him

> that there are two kings and two kingdoms in Scotland. There is Christ Jesus the King and his Kingdom the Kirk, whose subject King

James the Sixth is, and of whose Kingdom not a king, nor a head, but a member.[46]

Without considering the complexity of details, we may note that after James VI became King James I of England in the union of the Scottish and English crowns (upon the death of childless Elizabeth I in 1603) the tendency towards implementing Erastianism increased. The Scots Presbyterians saw this as an attempt to steal the headship of Christ over his Kirk. Episcopalian government was once again gradually imposed on the Scottish Kirk. This lasted until the famous reforming Presbyterian general assembly of 1638, which was a part of the broader English Puritan struggle against the "divine right" monarchical tyranny of the Stuarts. King James had written *Basilikon Doron* to defend absolute monarchy, and his less politically astute son, Charles I, fully shared his father's absolutist views on monarchical rights.

The covenanting movement was in full process at this time in Scotland with the adoption in 1638, of the National Covenant by all classes of the people to protect their church and its worship, and to acknowledge Christ's lordship over all the nation. Many of the people signed in their own blood. The attempt by Charles I and Archbishop Laud to impose the Anglican liturgy on the simpler worship of the Scottish Kirk led to armed resistance in Scotland.

To meet this crisis, Charles had to summon Parliament for the first time in many years, to finance a war against his rebellious Scottish subjects. This "Short Parliament" being pro-Puritan, and thus in favor of the actions of the Scottish nation, resisted the king. He dissolved Parliament, but soon had to call the fateful "Long Parliament" into session. The English Puritans took control of it and eventually through a civil war overturned the throne and established the Commonwealth.

This "Long Parliament" summoned the Westminster Assembly of Divines (which is discussed next chapter) to propose a statement of theological belief and form of church polity for the entire British kingdom. The result was the Westminster Confession of Faith. The Westminster Standards were adopted after much debate (particularly over the form of church government). Bishops were abolished and

Presbyterian polity was proclaimed. The headship of Christ was asserted (chap. 25) as was liberty of conscience (chap. 20).

One of the commissioners to the Westminster Assembly from the Church of Scotland was Samuel Rutherford, who published *Lex, Rex* ("The Law and the King") during the meetings of the assembly in the 1640s. In the line of Melville, he argued for two kingdoms, asserting that the king was not the law, but rather subject to God's law and obligated to the "fountain-power" of the people, who have the right and duty to overthrow him for abuse of the power they have delegated to him. He wrote:

> . . . for the fountain-power [scil. of government] remaineth most eminently in the people. 1. Because they give it to the king *ad modum recipientis*, and with limitations; therefore it is unlimited in the people, and bounded and limited in the king, and so less in the king than in the people.[47]

The general assembly of the Church of Scotland ratified the Westminster documents in 1647 and the Scottish Parliament approved them in 1649. But the documents never really became operative in England owing to the Parliament's combination of congregationalist sympathy and lingering Erastian tendencies to subordinate the church to the now "Puritan" state.

As happened so frequently during the century and a half following the Scottish Reformation, the situation was again reversed from Presbyterian polity to Episcopacy after the restoration of King Charles II in 1660.

> In 1669 the Act c. 2, the Act of Supremacy, once more asserted the Royal supremacy over all persons and in ecclesiastical matters. The famous Test Act of 1681 c. 6, was introduced to require the renunciation of the National Covenant and the Solemn League and Covenant by all persons in positions of public trust and to assert the Royal supremacy. In all this the Westminster Confession was not mentioned.[48]

For a number of years, especially in the 1670s and 1680s, the most fervently Presbyterian element of the Church of Scotland, the

Covenanters, endured severe governmental persecution because of their refusal to renounce the covenants and accept Episcopal government and admit the authority of civil powers over the church. In the words of the Covenanter, John Brown in *The Banders Disbanded* (1681), "The magistrates' power is neither subject nor subordinate to the ecclesiastic nor to be confounded with it, but is specifically distinct from it and co-ordinate therewith."[49] When one looks at the persecution that the Covenanters from time to time endured—including prison, torture, and death—the question arises as to why people would go to such extremes over theories of church polity.

For these people, the question of church polity was directly and inextricably related to what they deemed to be a life and death question involving eternal issues: "the crown rights of Jesus Christ" over his church. As Ian Doyle has explained:

> . . . for them any acknowledgement of royal or civil authority in things spiritual and ecclesiastical, was part of a vicious endeavor to dethrone Christ the King. Rather than that, exile and imprisonment, a stake by the Solway, a scaffold in the Grassmarket would be willingly accepted: nor, from what we know of the character and intentions of the last Stuart kings, can we say that their scruples were without reason.[50]

Covenanting Ideas and the "Glorious Revolution"

To a fair degree, the main principles contended for by the Covenanters were won in the final phase of the seventeenth-century English Revolution, known as the "Glorious Revolution" (1688), in which Catholic King James II (VII of Scotland) had to flee and was replaced on the British throne by his Protestant daughter Mary and her husband, William of Orange. The "Whig" political justification for declaring the throne of James II vacant appears to owe something to Scottish arguments of Knox and Melville and Rutherford, and perhaps even of the Covenanters, who declared the prince to be in covenant with God and the people. He was bound by the law of the covenant, for the abuse of which he could justly be deposed.

Though the intellectual lineage of these ideas is not without complexity and dispute, a strong influence upon John Locke seems quite probable. He was studying at the boys' school in Westminster Abbey while the Westminster Assembly was in progress, during which time Rutherford's *Lex, Rex* came out. He appears to draw upon Scottish (and French Huguenot) Calvinist concepts,[51] though in conjunction with possibly more significant elements that were not Calvinist. Thus Locke expressed the legitimacy of civil resistance in non-theological, strictly political terms of popular sovereignty and human rights. Buchanan and Althusius, as we have seen, were already pointing in this direction.

The covenantal Presbyterian arguments were specifically stated by the Scottish Parliament in its Claim of Right of 1689 c. 28, stating that James VII (James II of England) had forfeited the right to the Scottish crown and the throne had become vacant, because:

> By the advyce of wicked and evill Counsellers invade the fundamentall Constitution of this Kingdome And altered it from a legall limited monarchy to ane Arbitrary Despotick power and in a public proclamation asserted ane absolute power to cass annull and dissable all the lawes particularly arrainging the lawes Establishing the protestant Religion and to the violation of the lawes and liberties of the Kingdome.[52]

The first Scottish Parliament under the reign of William and Mary abolished prelacy in 1689, and in 1690 repealed earlier acts that had been prejudicial to Presbyterian polity and ecclesiastical liberty, reinstated deposed covenanting ministers, and once again officially ratified the Westminster Confession of Faith and Presbyterian church government.[53]

Historically and legally speaking, the next major phase in the relationship of the Church of Scotland with the state came with the union of the Scottish and English Parliaments in 1707. Various acts were passed in 1706, confirming tne Westminster Confession of Faith and Presbyterian government, requiring subscription of the confession by professors in the universities, and providing for "future sovereigns on their accession to take an oath to preserve inviolate this settlement of the Protestant religion and Presbyterian Church government."[54]

Parliamentary Union of Scotland and England: Later Problems

Although the Presbyterian polity seemed firmly established, serious problems were later to arise in spite of the 1706 Presbyterian "Act of Security," owing to the difference in understanding of basic church-state relations between the Scots Presbyterians and English Episcopalians. Nearly all of the later splits in the Church of Scotland would directly or indirectly stem from this difference of view (with the English Erastian view tending at times to be intruded into the church life of Scotland). MacAuley seems to have been correct in tracing all splits from the 1733 Secession down to the 1843 Disruption (when nearly half of the Scottish Church left the establishment over state-enforced lay patronage in pastoral elections) to the 1711 Act of Patronage, passed not long after the union of Parliaments.[55] This act in turn reflected the parliamentary and judicial predominance of the English Erastian theory over the quite different Scottish Presbyterian theory.

Lyall points out that the Scottish Presbyterian understanding of church-state relations was:

> that the General Assembly Act 1592, the Confession of Faith Ratification Act 1690, the Protestant Church and Presbyterian Church Act 1706 and all the others had merely recognized an already existing, self-existent and self-regulating community separate from the State and not requiring State sanction for the validity of its institutions and decisions. But in the then prevalent political requirements of monolithic authority, such an argument would not have been put. The theory of the single sovereign from whom all power is drawn, expressed in Hobbe's *Leviathan*, and later in the theory of John Austin, was in the ascendant. . . .
>
> The Church was increasingly seen as subject to the laws of the State. . . . The Disruption of the Church in 1843 was the direct result

of the collision of such a theory of the monolithic State with the idea of the independent Church which had earlier been expressed to a degree in Andrew Melville's *Second Book of Discipline*.[56]

Similarity of Presbyterian and Catholic Church-State Views?

At the time of the 1843 Disruption of the established Church of Scotland, those who left the Auld Kirk to form the Free Church of Scotland denied the right of the civil government to interfere in the appointment of ministers, while most of those who stayed either accepted it or at least were not prepared to leave over it. With considerable insight, the then current Roman Catholic Cardinal Manning of England noted the remarkable similarity of the Presbyterian "Free Church" views of church-state relations with those of the traditional Roman Catholic Church.[57]

Although Taylor Innes, a nineteenth-century expert on church-state relations in Scotland, replied to Cardinal Manning, and pointed out great differences between the Presbyterian and Roman Catholic views,[58] still the cardinal had a point that both Catholics (from whose conciliar tradition Calvin and Knox and Buchanan learned so much by way of John Major) and Presbyterians were firmly agreed in denying state control of the church.

During the public discussions preceding the 1843 Church Disruption (which split and severely weakened the influence of the Reformed faith in Scotland, by causing it soon to lose control of education and of laws benefitting the poor), Professor Ferrier expressed very clearly the ideal church-state understanding of the old Scottish Presbyterians. Ferrier, by the way, did not approve of leaving the Church of Scotland as the proper means to solve the problem. He wrote:

> If it be true (and who can doubt it) that the General Assembly is our old Scottish Parliament existing under the *phasis* in which it translated ecclesiastical business, then it is obvious that it is responsible to no higher authority, that no higher authority than itself exists; our

> Scottish Parliament is abolished *quoad civilia;* but it was never abolished *quoad sacra*. It still exists for the transaction of ecclesiastical business. Let the Parliament of England look to it.[59]

Of course, the British Parliament did not see the problem in this light, and so did not "look" to the general assembly of the Church of Scotland. In retrospect from the Covenanter viewpoint this was part of the price Scotland unwittingly paid for union with the more populous and influential England, whose rather different understanding of church-state relations had permeated the thought of its legislature and judiciary. However, later parliamentary acts in the last third of the nineteenth century would rectify matters for traditional Presbyterian polity in Scotland by abolishing the lay patronage act.[60]

Although it took centuries to order matters in its own house, the Reformed Church of Scotland made a deep and wide impact on concepts and practices of religious liberty and church-state relations far beyond Scotland. In the words of Harold Laski:

> . . . the vital conception of the two kingdoms, separate and distinct, was put forward in the first epoch of Scottish Presbyterian history by Andrew Melville; and it is safe to say that the attempt thus to define the limits of authorities basically conceived as distinct is the special contribution of Presbyterianism to the theory of political freedom.[61]

Notes

[1] Pierre Imbart de La Tour, *Les Origines de la Reforme*, 4 vol. (Paris: Dido et c^ie^, 1905-35), vol. 4: *Calvin et l'Institution Chretienne*, p. 117.

[2] John Knox, quoted by G. D. Henderson, *Presbyterianism* (Aberdeen: The University Press, 1954), p. 59.

[3] See James Baird, *Thunder Over Scotland*.

[4] Richard L. Greaves, *Theology and Revolution in the Scottish Reformation: Studies in the Thought of John Knox* (Grand Rapids: Eerdmans and Christian University, 1980), p. 116.

[5] Ibid., p. 118.

[6] See ibid., pp. 120, 121.

[7] Arthur H. Williamson, *Scottish National Consciousness in the Age of James VI: The Apocalypse, the Union and the Shaping of Scotland's Public Culture* (Edinburgh: John Donald, 1979), pp. 19, 20, 146.

[8] Francis Lyall, *Of Presbyters and Kings: Church and State in the Law of Scotland* (Aberdeen: Aberdeen University Press, 1980), pp. 9, 13.

[9] Greaves, *Theology and Revolution*, p. 149.

[10] Ibid., pp. 124, 125.

[11] Lyall, *Of Presbyters and Kings*, p. 13.

[12] The Scots Confession of 1560, Article XVIII.

[13] Lyall, *Of Presbyters and Kings*, pp. 13, 14.

[14] See edition by James K. Cameron, *The First Book of Discipline* (Edinburgh: The Saint Andrew Press, 1972).

[15] Lyall, *Of Presbyters and Kings*, p. 14.

[16] Cameron, *First Book of Discipline*, p. 95.

[17] Ibid., pp. 88, 89.

[18] Ibid., p. 88 n. 10.

[19] Scots Confession, preface.

[20] David Laing, ed., *Works of John Knox*, 6 vols. (New York: AMS Press, 1966), 3:166.

[21] Ibid., p. 64.

[22] Greaves, *Theology and Revolution*, p. 21.

[23] Bannatyne, *Memoriales*, p. 99, quoted in ibid., pp. 6, 7.

[24] J. H. S. Burleigh, *A Church History of Scotland* (London: Oxford University Press, 1960), p. 185.

[25] Greaves, *Theology and Revolution*, p. 126.

[26] See John Ponet, *A Short Treatise of Politic Power*, reprinted in Winthrop S. Hudson, *John Ponet (1516?-1556), Advocate of Limited Monarchy* (Chicago: University of Chicago Press, 1942), and Christopher Goodman, *How Superior Powers Ought to Be Obeyed of Their Subjects, and Wherein They May Lawfully by God's Word Be Disobeyed and Resisted* (Geneva, 1558).

[27] John Knox, *Faithful Admonition of 1554* and *An Answer, to a Great Number of Cavillations of 1558*.

[28] Greaves, *Theology and Revolution*, p. 18.

[29] Ibid.

[30] Ibid., pp. 155, 156. For examples, see Question IV of Samuel Rutherford's *Lex, Rex*, which lists typical Old Testament passages concerning the making and deposition of kings by the people, such as Judg. 7:22; 9:6; 11:8, 11; II Sam. 12:1; 16:18; I Kings 16; II Kings 14:21; II Chron. 23:3; Deut. 17:14, 15; etc.

[31] Reprinted by Sprinkle Publishing Company, Harrisonburg, Virginia, 1980.

[32] See Quentin Skinner, *The Foundations of Modern Political Thought* (Cambridge: Cambridge University Press, 1978), 2:338, 346.

[33] Ibid., p. 341.

[34] Williamson, *Scottish National Consciousness*, p. 108.

[35] Quoted in Lyall, *Of Presbyters and Kings*, p. 15.

[36] Ibid.

[37] Ibid., p. 16.

[38] Ibid.

[39] See Thomas McCrie, *Life of Andrew Melville*, vol. 2.

[40] Lyall, *Of Presbyters and Kings*, p. 17.

[41] Gordon Donaldson, *The Scottish Reformation* (Cambridge: Cambridge University Press, 1960), and the review by A. C. Cheyne in *Scottish Journal of Theology*, 16:78-88.

[42] See discussion in James Kirk, *The Second Book of Discipline* (Edinburgh: The Saint Andrew Press, 1980), pp. 13-28.

[43] Lyall, *Of Presbyters and Kings*, p. 17.

[44] Kirk, *Second Book of Discipline*, p. 58.

[45] James Walker, *The Theology and Theologians of Scotland: 1560-1750* (Edinburgh: Knox Press, 1872, 1982), pp. 127-56, "The Headship of Christ and Erastianism."

[46] Quoted in Burleigh, *Church History of Scotland*, pp. 204, 205.

[47] Samuel Rutherford, *Lex, Rex* (Harrisonburg, Va.: Sprinkle Publications, 1980, reprint), p. 82.

[48] Lyall, *Of Presbyters and Kings*, p. 19.

[49] Banders, quoted in Ian B. Doyle, "The Doctrine of the Church in the Later Covenanting Period," in *Reformation and Revolution*, ed. Duncan Shaw (Edinburgh: The Saint Andrew Press, 1967), p. 230.

[50] Doyle in Shaw, *Reformation and Revolution*, p. 234.

[51] See Skinner, *Foundations*, pp. 338-48.

[52] Lyall, *Of Presbyters and Kings*, p. 19.

[53] For details of the changeover from Episcopacy to Presbyterianism after 1688, see Burleigh, *Church History of Scotland*, pp. 261-85 and William Ferguson, *Scotland: 1689 to the Present, The Edinburgh History of Scotland*, vol. 4 (Edinburgh:Oliver and Boyd, 1968), pp. 1-35.

[54] Lyall, *Of Presbyters and Kings*, p. 21.

[55] As quoted in Harold J. Laski, *Studies in the Problem of Sovereignty* (London: Oxford University Press, 1917), pp. 33, 34.

[56] Lyall, *Of Presbyters and Kings*, p. 22.

[57] Laski, *Problem of Sovereignty*, pp. 49, 51.

[58] Ibid., p. 50. Presbyterian theorists maintained that their Reformed "two-kingdoms" concept differed from the Roman Catholic "two-kingdoms" theory, which they alleged had an implicit tendency for the church to assert control over the state. They also differed from the traditional Lutheran "two-kingdoms" idea, which the Reformed believed made too great a dichotomy between religion and state, with an implicit tendency for state to assert control over the church.

[59] James F. Ferrier, *Church and State* (1848), quoted in George E. Davie, *The Democratic Intellect in Scotland* (Edinburgh: The University Press, 1961), p. 307.

[60] See Lyall, *Of Presbyters and Kings*, pp. 23-84 for details.

[61] Laski, *Problem of Sovereignty*, p. 49.

4

Calvinism in England: The Puritan Struggle and Its Results

THE PROTESTANT REFORMATION in general succeeded in countries where there had not been an earlier amicable agreement between the secular authorities and the pope.

> Where it proved possible to arrange such Concordats, the governments involved—as in France and Spain—tended to remain faithful to the Catholic Church throughout the Reformation. But where the disputes over Annates, appointments and appeals remained unresolved—as in England, Germany and Scandanavia—the pressures on the Papacy continued to build up. Even before Luther's protestations began to be heard outside Germany, it is clear that these pressures had already come almost to breaking-point.[1]

The English Reformation

Along these lines, Chadwick has explained in broad terms the operative political motivations involved in the English Reformation: "It might be said broadly that in England, and in Denmark, the

Reformation came because limitation of the power of the Church was necessary to the further development of efficient government. . . . Before the Reformation began, the kings of Spain and France partially satisfied their need to control the Church."[2] The kings of England had not up to this time been able to control the church. Henry VII and Henry VIII however were very strong kings, and thus the stage was set for serious conflict with the church. This conflict surfaced during the reign of Henry VIII.

The unique viewpoint of Henry VIII and the unusual conflict, compromise, and settlement that occurred under him make the later Puritan reaction a logically understandable consequence. In the eyes of large numbers of earnest English Protestants, the Henrician settlement meant that the English Church was (to borrow Hetherington's description) but a half-reformed church.[3] A large party of people throughout the nation would soon set about the task of completing the work of Reformation, as they understood it. An important segment of this reforming party would in later years come to be known, rather derisively at first, as Puritans. We must look at the settlement of Henry VIII and his immediate successors in order to understand what this influential party wanted to "purify."

Henry VIII was basically satisfied with traditional Catholic doctrine and liturgy. He was opposed to Lutheran doctrine and earned himself the title given him by the pope "Defender of the Faith" for his writings criticizing Luther's views on the sacraments. Thus while not desiring doctrinal and liturgical reformation, Henry did want to see legal changes in the relationships between monarch, pope, and church. Matters came to a head in Henry's desire for a male heir to the throne. He wished to divorce his wife, Catherine of Aragon, on the rather tenuous grounds that she had been contracted to his elder brother Arthur. He wanted Pope Clement VII to grant a divorce and allow him to marry Anne Boleyn, through whom he hoped to have a male heir. It is possible that he had a case according to canon law, but Clement VII would have deeply offended Emperor Charles V, nephew of Catherine of Aragon had he granted Henry's wish, and hence he refused.

From 1529 to 1534 through the courts, Parliament, and convocation, Henry took various actions by which "the . . . legal rights and duties of the Pope were transferred to the crown. In [1534] the Act of Supremacy declared that the King was supreme head of the Church of England. . . ."[4] In the later 1530s monasteries were suppressed to the financial enrichment of the crown and the territorial enrichment of gentry and noble families. "In 1539 the repressive Act of Six Articles attempted to vindicate the Catholic faith of the king by decreeing savage penalties for denial of transubstantiation, private masses, private confession, or the need for clerical celibacy, and shocked Protestants hopeful about English progress."[5]

There can be no doubt that there were many in the land who did desire a thorough Protestant Reformation, and who were disappointed by Henry's failure to carry it through. It would be a serious misunderstanding to write off the English Reformation—even that segment of it that was bounded by the reign of Henry VIII—as merely a political, economic, and legal matter. While those factors were crucial, strong pro-Reformation religious currents were sweeping across the country. Even before Henry's open moves against the pope in 1529, Tyndale's English translation of the New Testament had been smuggled into England and, along with some of Tyndale's popular theological writings, was creating an atmosphere desirous of reform. Lutheran thought as mediated by Tyndale and many others had a large, sympathetic constituency prepared to receive it in the ranks of those influenced by Wycliffe's Bible-preaching Lollards. In the early 1520s Coverdale, Latimer, Bilney, and others at Cambridge were studying with appreciation the writings of Luther. The number of those who favored serious religious reformation was growing and hailed with great hope the reign of the godly boy-king Edward VI (reigned 1547-53), since "at last the gates were open to the reforming party."[6]

Under the guidance of the proreform Protector Somerset and Archbishop Cranmer (who now held essentially Protestant theological views), as well as a host of others in influential positions in church and state who favored Reformation, the king and Parliament moved the church in a much more decidedly Protestant direction. The reformed liturgy in the prayer books of 1549 and 1552 may certainly be considered a classical monument of the Reformation, although it still contained many medieval Catholic elements, which the Scot John Knox (one of Edward VI's court chaplains) termed "mishmash."

Much to the grief of the reform party, the Calvinist boy-king died in 1553, long before he had had time to carry out the thorough reform of England he sincerely desired. Chadwick states the national and ecclesiastical situation at that time succinctly: "In 1553 England was by no means a Protestant country. It was made more nearly Protestant by the reign of Queen Mary."[7]

Without tarrying over the details of Mary's reign, we must note that she vigorously—but unsuccessfully—and indeed counter-productively attempted to restore full Roman Catholicism in England. Her executions of respected Protestant leaders "baptized the English Reformation in blood, and drove into English minds the fatal association of ecclesiastical tyranny with the See of Rome. . . . Five years before, the Protestant cause was identified with church robbery, destruction, irreverence, religious anarchy. It was now beginning to be identified with virtue, honesty, and loyal English resistance to a half-foreign government."[8] Another unintended benefit of the Marian persecution to the future English Reformation was the dispersal of Protestant scholars from England to the Continent, where they found shelter with leading Reformers (especially, though not exclusively, of Calvinist opinion) from whom they learned and by whose vision they were stirred to deeper reform when they could safely return to England and Scotland after the death of childless Mary in 1558.

Edward was Calvinist, Protestant; Mary was Roman Catholic, while her sister, Elizabeth, who succeeded her, seemed somewhere between the two. Probably she was most like her father, Henry VIII, and wanted essentially Catholic doctrine and practice without the control of the pope. Again, we need not outline the major events of her long and important reign (1558-1603) to assess its ecclesiastical consequences, which were so important in the development of the Puritan party.

Though Elizabeth's own inclinations seem to have been rather traditionally Catholic, soon after her accession to the throne the pope declared her illegitimate so that Elizabeth felt forced to uphold Protestantism in some form as the support to her throne. Some important reforms were carried through in the early years of her reign: bishops loyal to the pope were deprived of their offices; the revised Book of Common Prayer was ratified by act of Parliament; and in 1562 the

Thirty-Nine Articles of Religion reached their definitive form. In the view of the reform-minded Puritans, however, what was not reformed was of more significance than what was reformed. Yet "Queen Elizabeth and her advisers aimed at securing a compromise; a middle road between the jangling parties which divided the kingdom; a 'golden mediocrity,' if like Archbishop Matthew Parker one believed moderation to be right; a 'leaden mediocrity,' a 'mingle-mangle,' as some of the disciples of the Swiss preferred to call it."[9]

Who Were the Puritans?

We have made frequent reference to a reform party in the Church of England known as Puritans. A great deal of academic debate has gone on concerning the definition of Puritan, and two or three writers have taken the unlikely position (in which they have not been followed by the mainstream) that the term itself is useless and should be dropped.[10] Christopher Hill, the great scholar of seventeenth-century English history, has an entire chapter devoted to this complex question.[11] He summarizes:

> . . . there was in England in the two or three generations before the civil war a body of opinion which can usefully be labelled as Puritan. There was a core of doctrine about religion and Church government, aiming at purifying the Church from inside. This doctrine for various reasons won the support of a substantial and growing group of laymen. It is not to be identified with either Presbyterianism or Independency. . . . [Puritan] thought was not monolithic, but they adopted comparable attitudes . . . and these attitudes seem to have appealed to the larger circle of lay opinion which we can conveniently describe as Puritan, the body of opinion without which the civil war could never have been fought.[12]

Puritanism therefore has to be considered in terms of both religious and political ramifications, for as Christopher Hill has said elsewhere: "The body of ideas which has to be called 'Puritan,' for want of a better word, was a philosophy of life, an attitude to the universe, which by no means excluded secular interests. . . .

'Puritanism' in the seventeenth century was not in the narrow sense restricted to religion and morals, any more than science or history were narrowly 'secular' subjects."[13]

At the heart of the Puritan controversy with the Elizabethan Church settlement was their Calvinist inspired "regulative principle," according to which all spheres of life—church, home, state, and vocation—are to be specifically regulated according to the commands and principles of the Word of God. The Puritans were purists in worship because they believed that what was not specifically enjoined in Scripture as regards religious ceremonies was forbidden. "The Calvinists contended that all things done in church must have positive warrant in Scripture, and on this ground attacked the English Prayer Book and the polity of the Elizabethan settlement."[14]

Mitchell, the distinguished nineteenth-century historian of the Westminster Assembly, rightly points out that

> the points of difference between the Puritans and those who fail to be distinguished from them in the Reformed Church of England seem at first to have been few in number, and of minor importance. . . . So far again as concerned matters of worship and church polity, the only expression at variance with the principle of Puritanism in the Articles of the Church was the first clause of the XXth Article, asserting the power of the Church to decree rites and ceremonies. This clause was not contained in the corresponding article as framed in the time of Edward VI; and the Puritans strenuously contended it had been foisted in, somewhat inconsiderately, in the time of Queen Elizabeth.[15]

Hetherington outlines these differences as they were brought up in the convocation of 1562:

> Six alterations were proposed [i.e., to the prayer book], to the following purport: The abrogation of all holidays, except Sabbaths, and those relating to Christ,—that in prayer the minister should turn his face to the people, so that they might hear and be edified,—that the ceremony of the cross in baptism might be omitted, that the sick and aged might not be compelled to kneel at the communion,—that the partial use of the surplice might be sufficient,—and that the use of organs be laid aside.[16]

Mitchell's assessment concerning the relative closeness of the early Puritans and the first Church of England prelates is correct: "Many of the first Elizabethan bishops agreed with them, and would willingly have abandoned the obnoxious ceremonies if the queen would have consented."[17]

Many of the Elizabethan bishops and some of those under James I as well shared the doctrinal Calvinism of the Puritans, and indeed this stream of Augustinian-Calvinist thought has never ceased to be represented in the Church of England in varying degrees in different centuries. Yet in the time of Elizabeth another school of theology arose in conscious opposition to Puritan Calvinism, which defended the mediating Anglican establishment in a very powerful way in part through the reintroduction of Aristotelian Thomistic natural law theology by Richard Hooker (1553/54-1600) in his epoch-making *Laws of Ecclesiastical Polity*.

> In order to defend the Anglican Establishment Hooker circumvented both the Puritan appeal to Scripture and the Catholic appeal to Church tradition by going behind both to the primary source of authority: natural law, which is implanted in people's minds by God and comes to full expression in the state. The voice of the people is the voice of God, but is articulated through the civil magistrate. While Hooker held that Scripture contained what is necessary for salvation still the law of nature was primary. As times change, specific laws [including Scripture] can be changed, though always in accordance with fundamental natural law. Thus the church cannot be held subject to the letter of Scripture or of tradition; it is free to adjust itself to its own historical context.[18]

In years to come this revival of natural law concepts as a central theological authority would lead to tensions among British Protestants over the nature and relationship of divine and human laws. Hence in addition to strictly liturgical matters, part of what the later Puritans—and in particular the Westminster Assembly—would be contending against theologically was this sort of revived natural law theology, which in their opinion tended to focus on the constructions of the mind of man rather than the revelation of God (though this criticism would have doubtlessly been rejected by the followers of Hooker).

Some of the problems connected with the granting of natural law a central place in theology would appear over a century later in English deism and in the Continental secularist Enlightenment, which drew so much of its original inspiration from English deism. In this later movement, nature would attempt to destroy grace, but such an outcome would never have been conceived of, much less intended, by Hooker and his anti-Puritan followers.

The Puritan Revival

As we continue considering Puritanism under its religious aspects, we note that its emphasis on the regulative principle was essentially an outcome of the Calvinist desire to be God-centered and to do all for his glory. How better, the Puritans asked, can one be theocentric than by placing his Word above all else as the interpretative principle through which one sees and orders all reality? How consistently they were able to carry this out in various spheres is still debated, but nonetheless their intentions were clear. As a historical phenomenon the question of why a large and influential segment of the population of England and Scotland was consciously striving to bring the various spheres of life under the regulation of God's Word, as they understood it, is an important one. Although we must later consider crucial economic, social, and cultural factors contributing to the rise and development of Puritanism, as with the parent Protestant Reformation, the movement can be understood as nothing less than a religious revival.

Iain Murray has demonstrated that the contemporary Puritans themselves certainly saw it in these terms:

> There was recovered at the time of the Reformation belief in what may be called revival Christianity, and the attention which the Puritans who followed gave to this area of truth profoundly influenced the following centuries. . . .[19]
>
> The Reformation, and still more, Puritanism, have been considered from many aspects but it has been too often overlooked that the main features of these movements, as, for instance, the extensiveness of their influence, the singular position given to Scripture and

> the transformation in character of the morally careless, are all effects of revival. When the Holy Spirit is poured out in a day of power the result is bound to affect whole communities and even nations. Conviction of sin, an anxiety to possess the Word of God, and dependence upon those which glorify God in man's salvation, are inevitable consequences.[20]

Christopher Hill speaks in a similar way about the necessity of recognizing deep spiritual motivations in explaining the English Civil War:

> The civil war, then cannot be explained merely by looking at M.P.'s. Men did not die and kill one another for four years over issues which can be satisfactorily analyzed by a method evolved for a period in which there were no serious political disagreements. The civil war was fought about issues of principle which roused large numbers of men to heroic activity and sacrifice.[21]

Nonetheless, it was widely recognized in the seventeenth century as well as in twentieth-century historiography that the Puritan movement had deep political ramifications.[22] Hill says, "Puritan" came to be used to describe almost any opponent of the court. A pamphlet published in 1643, allegedly by the Venetian ambassador, described three factions in England—Protestant, Catholic, and Puritan. The last named "is the most potent, consisting of some bishops, all the gentry and commonalty."[23] Puritan political opposition to the established church settlement and thus to the court was one of the strong factors leading to the English Civil War out of which came the Westminster Confession of Faith.

Seventeenth-Century English Revolution

Stephen Gardiner, the great nineteenth-century historical authority on the seventeenth-century Puritan and Civil War period, on which he wrote eighteen important volumes, brought into prominence the phrase "Puritan Revolution" to describe the 1640s Civil War. Few scholars today would accept this terminology since it implies an over-simplification that neglects very important economic and social factors, which both Puritan and non-Puritan writers of the seventeenth century recognized themselves.[24] Some Marxist scholars (such as Professor Archangelsky of Leningrad) have done valuable work here and have manifested appreciation of the social and political accomplishments of the seventeenth-century Puritan movement.

Without in any sense denying the vitally significant religious factors contributing to the English Revolution, this phenomenon must be set in its broader European socio-economic and political context:

> The whole of Europe faced a crisis in the mid-seventeenth century, which expressed itself in a series of breakdowns, revolts, and civil wars. The sixteenth century had seen the opening up of America and of new trade routes to the Far East; a sudden growth of population all over Europe, and a monetary inflation which was also all-European. These phenomena are related (both as effect and cause) to the rise of capitalist relations within feudal society and a consequent regrouping of social classes.[25]

The seventeenth-century scholar, Harrington, interpreted the Civil War largely in terms of shifts in control of property among the various classes of England: "Harrington's theory of history [holds] that changes in the balance of property must lead to political change unless legislative action not in conflict with economic tendencies modif[y] this determinism."[26] Hill deals with this question in detail in chapters 2 and 5 of *Puritanism and Revolution*. As he shows, some have interpreted part of the widespread support for Puritan resistance to the Stuart kings in terms of a rising gentry, eager for more property, while others see it in precisely the opposite way: the gentry was declining economically and feared losing what it had. Whichever of the two theories is correct, the following cannot be denied:

> Fear that Charles I was going to attempt in England the policy of resuming church lands which he had initiated in Scotland and Ireland caused many gentlemen to support Parliament. . . . A century and a half after the dissolution, James II, in introducing his Declaration of Indulgence, felt obliged to say explicitly that he had no

> intention of following the grant of toleration, to Catholics by an attempt to recover monastic lands. It was still a real political issue, and had been for the intervening 150 years.[27]

Earlier we mentioned that in the mid-sixteenth century there were relatively moderate differences between most of the Puritans and the leading Elizabethan bishops. As time went on, the differences were perceived to be far more radical, and conflict increased in intensity and frequency, often in relationship to international events affecting the Catholic-Protestant "balance of power" in Europe.

> Down to 1589 the Earl of Leicester saw to it that learned Puritan preachers were promoted in the Church, or gave them large stipends out of his own purse. But after Leicester's death, and with the simplification of foreign policy issues after 1588, the influence of Puritanism declined. It grew again as a new threat to Protestantism appeared in the Thirty Years War. Foreign policy [was] closely bound up with religion. . . .[28]

In addition to ceremonial and purely theological concerns (such as the Calvinist Puritan predestinarianism, which was being increasingly opposed by some—though by no means all—Anglican leaders in the early seventeenth century), there was fierce theological and political contention over the concept of bishops. Many Anglicans (though again, certainly not all) believed that bishops were lineal successors of the apostles, were thus a separate order from regular ministers, and were essential to the very existence of the church. The Puritans held that according to the New Testament (and to Jerome and other church scholars) bishops were the same as elders and thus were merely ministers. They believed that apostolic succession meant merely faithfulness to the teachings of apostolic doctrine and practice. Instead of prelatic government of the church, the Puritans (for the most part) held to representative government by presbytery (though as we shall soon see, a number of Puritans favored Independency and others favored bishops).

Far from being a matter of merely ecclesiastical or antiquarian interest, vital political issues of intense interest to the civil government were involved in this conflict of interpretation. This was debated through the long years of the reign of Elizabeth I and reached a new intensity after the union of the crowns of England and Scotland in 1603, when James VI of Scotland became James I of Great Britain.

"No Bishop, No King"

James (VI) I, though coming from a Presbyterian country, had no use for Puritanism and Presbyterianism. They were in his view a serious threat to the absolute monarchy to which he was totally devoted. This very learned, though pedantic king, wrote a book—*Basilikon Doron*—extolling the unbounded powers of the absolute monarch as God's unquestionable requirement upon all flesh. His son, Charles I, held the same absolutist, "divine right" views. Both James and Charles Stuart believed that divine right bishops were a necessary governmental support to divine right kings. In this belief they were no different from most of the other European monarchs of their day. When James I scolded the Puritan leaders at the Hampton Court Conference (between the king and his Anglican bishops on one side and Puritan leaders on the other side) in 1604 with the maxim, "No Bishop, no King," he was speaking both logically (in terms of his own position) and in a certain sense, prophetically. The contemporary opponents of the Stuart monarchs—and especially the opponents of Charles I—were quick to point out the nonbiblical and noncommon-law basis of their absolutist policy. This criticism took a number of forms, but none perhaps was more influential than the allegation that the Stuarts had subverted the ancient freedoms guaranteed by the common law of England, through their innovative, centralizing courts, in which bishops had a part.

English Common Law: Truth and Myth

From the middle of the reign of Queen Elizabeth until the overthrow of Charles I, it was the contention of the Puritans—and many others, especially those in the rising commercial classes, the gentry and the lawyers—that the crown and its bishops were subverting the old common law system in order to thwart the liberties of the people in the interests of an enlarged, centralized power by means of such instruments as the Court of High Commission. Hill explains:

> The High Commission began to function as a regular court from the 1580's—when the threat from the Puritan radicals began to be taken seriously by the Government. . . . (Archbishop Whitgift in 1583) said . . . that the court was necessary because of the solidarity and influential support enjoyed, at least in certain areas, by Puritans; and the oath *ex officio* was essential because common law procedure was inadequate to overcome the difficulty of collecting enough evidence to secure convictions. . . .
>
> The over-riding powers of such a court were invaluable to the hierarchy. By the end of Elizabeth's reign bishops were trying to get separate commissions for their own dioceses, as a means of enforcing discipline; failing that, they frequently transferred cases from their own to the High Commission in order to ensure a successful prosecution.[29]

Yet these new, high-handed methods roused strong opposition, and would ultimately prove counterproductive for the crown:

> Opposition to the High Commission was thus a curious compound of interest and principle. Common lawyers, Puritans and printers disliked the Commission: so, too, did many rich litigants who utilized the law's delays. But it was also opposed by the growing body of lay opinion which resented the moral jurisdiction of clerics, or ecclesiastical censorship, or heavy fines, or all three.[30]

Thus the legal innovations of the royal administration were one of the main factors leading to irrevocable conflict between crown and Parliament. Sir Edward Coke (1552-1634), the great systematizer of English law, played a major role in this conflict:

> [Coke] systematized English law and in the process continued and extended the process of literalizing it, of adapting it to the needs of a commercial society. In so doing he had to challenge . . . arbitrary taxation and arbitrary arrest, paternal control over the economic life of the country. This brought the common law into conflict with the

prerogative and its courts, the Church and its courts; it was natural and inevitable that Coke should turn to the House of Commons for support as soon as he had failed to achieve his aims within the government.[31]

Hill has shown that there was a large element of myth in the contentions of the common lawyers and Puritans against the royal administration (such as Coke's making *Magna Charta* things about economic liberalism that were thoroughly anachronistic).[32] And Rosenstock-Huessy has shown that much of what was claimed as ancient Anglo-Saxon procedure was simply the general medieval European Christian heritage of biblically based ecclesiastical justice.[33] Nevertheless there was more than enough truth in the myth to play a major part in overturning the throne in the impending English Civil War.

The King: A Revolutionist?

The conflicts over subversion of personal liberties through the government's overriding common law brought to burning focus this charge of the common lawyers, Puritans, and commercial classes against the crown and its administration: the king was acting as a revolutionist against the people. Of course the implication of this charge was that such royal action might need to be restrained by action that would theoretically consider itself to be a conservative, counter revolution (though needless to say, this interpretation would not be accepted by supporters of the court or by most of Europe).[34]

Events Leading Up to the English Civil War

After the union of the crowns of England and Scotland in 1603, the Puritans had high hopes of better treatment under James I than under the late Elizabeth.

As [James VI (I)] proceeded on his way to take possession of his new kingdom, petitions for relief or indulgence were presented to him by the oppressed Puritans. . . . Chief among these petitions was the

> Millenary Petition—so designated . . . from its being signed by nearly a thousand [in reality about 800] ministers. . . . It was expressed in deferential and moderate language, and its prayer for relief might have been granted without the slightest danger to the church. . . .[35]

The result of this petition was the Hampton Court Conference, held in 1604, to which James I invited four leading Puritan scholars and ministers along with Archbishop Whitgift, eight bishops, and other Anglican Church officials. Instead of being a "calm judge," he was, as Mitchell has said, a "keen partisan." He dealt with the Puritans "with arrogance and coarseness" and deeply offended them.[36] He accused them of "aiming at a Scottish Presbytery, which agreeth with a monarchy as well as God with the devil. There Jack, and Tom, and Will, and Dick, shall meet and at their pleasure censure me and my council."[37] Finally he threatened Dr. Reynolds of Oxford and the other Puritan scholars: ". . . I will make them conform, or else I will harry them out of the land, or else do worse, hang them—that is all." However, out of this otherwise disappointing conference did come the authority to make the classical English translation of the Bible known as the "Authorized" or "King James' Version."

King Charles I (reigned 1625-49) was as unaware of, or perhaps as uninterested in, the deeper aspirations of the majority of his people as was his father, James I. He carried forward his father's harsh absolutism in church and state with even greater rigor—especially after the appointment of the very "high-church", extreme anti-Puritan and anti-Calvinist Archbishop Laud of Canterbury in 1633. Charles I, while sincere in his faith in divine right absolute monarchy, was not a very effective politician (though admittedly he was in circumstances that would have been difficult for the most accomplished statesman). Not many years would pass before it would be plain for all to see that Charles's intransigence and Laud's harsh persecutions, far from accomplishing the ends intended in subduing the Puritans, were counterproductively raising massive opposition and thus sealing the doom of royal absolutism. Of course from Charles I's perspective, he was merely defending national religious unity and divinely ordained royal right. Such opposing positions would only be settled by war.

Charles I had dissolved Parliament in 1628 and "endeavored for twelve years to govern without the advice of the Houses. To do this he had to arrogate increased Power to his Privy Council . . . and to surrender himself to the guidance of able but unscrupulous men, who thought to carry out in England the policy Richelieu had pursued with success in France, and make their master absolute. . . . [These men] like their master, lived in isolation, and were unconscious of the forces that were ranging themselves against them."[38]

Archbishop Laud was for years "the king's most confidential adviser in State as well as in Church affairs. . . . He used the powers of his high office and of the Courts of Star-Chamber and High Commission with a rigor and savagery unknown."[39] The growing congregation of the Massachusetts Bay Colony emigrated from England, beginning in 1628. Their numbers greatly increased after Laud was appointed in 1633 and began systematically persecuting Puritans.

Scottish Developments and the English Parliament

No action of Charles I and Laud had such devastating repercussions on the cause they stood for as their ill-fated attempt to impose a high church liturgy on Puritan, Presbyterian Scotland. Resentment in Scotland was already at a high pitch because of James I's forcing bishops on a largely unwilling Presbyterian populace some years before. Possibly many in Scotland might have ultimately favored Anglicanism had it not been forced on them from the outside. But as it was, Presbyterianism was naturally deemed patriotic, and Anglican prelacy looked upon as foreign tyranny.

Evidence would indicate that the Scottish Church historian Donald MacLean was right in noting that in Scotland the popular Presbyterian movement was a largely religious phenomenon, whereas the corresponding English movement, while also religious to a degree, was at the same time motivated by a number of political factors (as we have just discussed): "Besides, the causes of the Scots and English differed in origin and in their national ends. The ground of the Scottish quarrel was wholly religious, while the English quarrel sprang from questions of polity and constitutional politics."[40]

English history for the next decade would to a large degree

depend on the relationship of the pro-Puritan Parliament and army to the revived Scottish Presbyterians. The Scottish revival known as the Second Reformation was a powerful event that would deeply influence the history of the Western world. It too, as well as the earlier Protestant Reformation, would be powerful in setting back statist absolutism. (The American colonies and later United States of America can be understood as heirs of liberties achieved in the state-church balance won in the Scottish Second Reformation.)

Just as absolutist "divine right" monarchy was ultimately based on naturalistic principles, so the religious and civil liberties of the Scottish Second Reformation were based on an opposite philosophy: a God-centered approach to life, rooted in salvation in accordance with biblically derived principles of transcendent law superior to nature and thus standing judge over the political constructions of the mind of man.

When in 1637 the English civil authorities attempted to impose by force a Church of England type of liturgy onto the Church of Scotland, the reaction in retrospect is understandable. Riots resulted in Edinburgh. In the words of Mitchell, "But as King James had said long before, 'he knew not the stomach of that people,' and perhaps he recked not what a great conflagration this train he had laid was to light up."[41]

Hetherington describes in brief the reaction:

> The attempt provoked an instantaneous and determined resistance. A large portion of the nobility, nearly all the middle class, the whole of the ministers, and almost the entire body of the people, united in a solemn national covenant in defense of their religious liberties, resolved to peril life . . . rather than submit to the threatened violation of conscience. The King raised an army to subdue them by force, but shrunk from the perilous encounter, and framed an evasive truce. This abortive attempt almost exhausted his treasury, and compelled him reluctantly to call a Parliament, from which he hoped to procure supplies.[42]

As a continuation of the forces unleashed by the liturgical riots in Edinburgh followed by the signing of the National Covenant in February, 1638, the revived general assembly of the Church of

Scotland met in Glasgow in late 1638. It was filled with Presbyterian, anti-Anglican prelacy delegates, who elected Alexander Henderson as moderator (who would later be one of the six Scottish commissioners to the Westminster Assembly). This assembly—in face of the certain displeasure of the king—abolished bishops in Scotland, removed Episcopal legislation from the records, and reestablished Presbytery. This was followed by the First Bishops' War in which the king made an ineffective attempt to invade Scotland in order to resubjugate its church. In simple terms, the Scottish Covenanters had a larger and better army. After only token fighting, hostilities were ended "by the Pacification of Berwick, in terms of which the Covenanters agreed to disband their army in return for a promise from Charles to appoint an assembly to meet in Edinburgh in August 1639 to be immediately followed by a Parliament. Unwillingly he consented to the exclusion of the bishops from the assembly, but he encouraged them to hand in a new declinature, and he assured them of his intention to restore them when he could."[43]

Charles however instead of carrying out his promise, took the fateful step of calling an English Parliament, which he hoped would finance a second Bishops' War against Scotland.

> The "Short" Parliament proved intractable and was dissolved within a month. Taking advantage of the king's difficulties and weary of repeated prorogations the Scots Parliament met in defiance of the king and his commissioner, June 1640, ratified the acts of the assembly (i.e. of Glasgow). . . . In August a Covenanting army crossed the Tweed and occupied Newcastle and Durham, so compelling the king to summon the fateful "Long" Parliament (November 1640). Strongly Puritan and Presbyterian in sympathy. . . .[44]

The Long Parliament

The Long Parliament met from 1640 until it was expelled by Cromwell in 1652. It was made up of a majority of proliberty and pro-Puritan men, such as Pym, Hampden, Cromwell, and Selden. Though definitely Puritan in sympathy, it seems to have been divided into two parties, which MacCormack designates "moderate" (in preference to the older term "Presbyterian") and "radical" (which was much more anti-Monarchical).[45] As we shall later see, the cleavage of these two parties helps explain the inconsistent relationship of the Parliament with the Westminster Assembly.

At its very beginning the Long Parliament set up four committees to deal with what they considered the most urgent issues of the times: religious grievances, the affairs of Scotland and Ireland, civil grievances, and popery and popish plots. A vast number of petitions from all over the country began pouring into Parliament signed by thousands of citizens, urging various sorts of relief and reformation. Probably the most influential was one from the city of London, signed by about fifteen thousand persons, and generally termed "The Root and Branch Petition," on account of an expression occuring in its prayer, viz., "That the said government, with all its dependencies, roots and branches, may be abolished."[46]

After a plot against Parliament was discovered, a bill was passed: "That this present Parliament shall not be adjourned, prorogued, or dissolved, without their own consent." Parliament soon took the significant step of preparing to set up a military force "for the security of their liberties and of the Protestant religion."[47]

Another committee on religion was appointed with ten bishops, twenty lay peers, and Puritan ministerial advisers to study innovations in doctrine and the question of ritual, but nothing came of this committee. Bills passed in 1641 abolishing the Court of High Commission and the Star Chamber were signed by the king. Archbishop Laud and the king's right-hand man, the anti-Puritan Stafford, were committed to the Tower of London. A National Covenant (similar to the one in Scotland) was signed by Parliament in May 1641 and sent out to be subscribed by the whole kingdom, pledging further Protestant reformation and extirpation of popery. (This was done two years before the later, more famous "Solemn League and Covenant" suggested by Scotland.)

In December of 1641 the House of Commons presented the king the Grand Remonstrance, which specified religious grievances and asked for "a general synod of the most grave, pious, learned, and judicious divines of this island, assisted with some from foreign parts professing the same religion with us, who may consider of all things necessary for the peace and good government of the Church; and to represent the result of their consultations, to be allowed and confirmed, and to receive the stamp of authority."[48] Although the Grand Remonstrance was duly presented to the king, Rosenstock-Huessy suggests that it contained an exceptionally important political innovation, which was to set the trend for the future: ". . . [in] the Grand Remonstrance . . . the Lower House, for the first time in history, appealed 'downwards' to the people instead of upward to the King. . . ."[49]

The king refused to allow the meeting of this proposed synod, whereupon Parliament turned the bill into an ordinance, which convened the assembly by their own authority on June 12, 1643.

The Westminster Assembly

The ordinance makes it plain that this was not an ordinary ecclesiastical assembly or synod, but rather an advisory body to the Parliament. As the Scottish commissioner Robert Baillie described it: ". . . this is no proper Assembly, but a meeting called by the Parliament to advise them in what things they are asked. . . ."[50] Hetherington explains why under the political circumstances of the times, the Westminster Assembly had to assume this particular state-dependent form:

> It was neither a Convocation [i.e., Anglican], or a Presbyterian Synod or General Assembly; and it could not be either the one or the other, for the prelatic form of Church government had been abolished, and there was no other yet in existence. The true theory of the Westminster Assembly comprises two main elements;—there was a Christian Church in England, but not organized; and the civil power, avowing Christianity, had called an Assembly of Divines for the purpose of consulting together respecting those points of government and discipline which require the sanction of civil authority for their full efficiency. Such an Assembly could have been called only by a Christian civil magistrate; and only in a transition state of the Church, when disorganized, or not yet duly constituted. In such a state of matters, the problem to be solved was this: On what terms could a

> National Church be constituted, so as neither to encroach upon civil liberty, as the Papal and Prelatic Churches had done, nor to yield up those inherent spiritual rights, privileges, and liberties, which are essential to a Church of Christ?[51]

Carruthers properly summarizes the position of the members of the Westminster Assembly: "The divines were mere advisers, prohibited from exercising ecclesiastical authority or power. They were authorized to consider government and . . . duly tendered their advice."[52]

In the meantime political and military events with important ecclesiastical ramifications occurred, which caused Parliament to order the assembly to cease work on the Thirty-Nine Articles in order to prepare a confession of faith for the churches of the three kingdoms. There had already been considerable communication between the English Parliament and the Scottish Parliament and general assembly of the Church of Scotland, but without firm results. Now however because Parliament was going backward militarily in the contest with the king, they greatly needed the assistance of Scotland. J. A. R. Marriott, writing from an English viewpoint, stated that "Baillie is justified in taking credit to the Scots in coming to the assistance of a ruined cause" (commenting on Baillie, *Letters and Journals*, 2:99-100).[53] Warfield states the Scottish position:

> The Scots, indeed, had nothing to gain: from the alliance which was offered them, unless they gained security for their Church from future English interference; while on the other hand by entering into it they risked everything which they had at such great cost recovered for themselves. Their own liberties were already regained; the cause of Parliament in England, on the contrary, hung in the gravest doubt. It really was an act of high chivalry, to call it by no more sacred name, for them to cast in their lot at this crisis with the Parliament. . . ."[54]

At first, the English and Scots commissioners approached the proposed alliance from different perspectives. Baillie states, "The English were for a civil League, we for a religious Covenant."[55] In desiring a religious covenant:

> The Scots demanded nothing more than that the Parliament should explicitly bind itself to the course it was on its own loudly professing

> to be following, and had already declared in the ordinance [for example] by which it had called to its aid an advisory council of Divines, to be the object it was setting before itself in the reconstruction of the English Church. All that was asked of the Parliament, in point of fact, was thus, that it should give greater precision, and binding force under the sanction of a solemn covenant, to its repeatedly declared purpose.[56]

The English commissioners agreed to this "on the suggestion of Sir Harry Vane, that the two ideas might very properly be combined; and hence the bond of union between the two countries was so framed as to embrace both subjects, and received the appropriate designation of *The Solemn League and Covenant*."[57]

This document was written by Alexander Henderson, moderator of the general assembly of the Church of Scotland, and soon to be one of the influential Scottish commissioners to the Westminster Assembly. The Solemn League and Covenant is both theological and political; its theology is strong God-centered Calvinism with specific application to the great issues that molded individual and societal life in that day. It is infused with a sense of God's glory, providence, grace, and holy requirements; and at the same time, it is marked by an open confession of the sinfulness of man and unworthy response of the redeemed (see Article VI), and the necessity of taking specific and immediate individual and corporate reformatory action out of obedience to God.[58]

It is important to note in the history of thought that this kind of God-centered Calvinist theology led to individual and national liberty and civil rights in balance with necessary state authority. Samuel Rutherford, another of the Scottish commissioners to the Westminster Assembly, wrote a significant work—*Lex, Rex*—showing that the king (rex) is always under God's law (lex).

It is significant that the (Protestant) enemies of the Calvinists—particularly in England—were Arminians, whose theology represented a more man-centered approach, deemphasizing the sovereignty of God.[59] The practical results of Arminianism for politics (though certainly not the intent of the Arminians) was like the results of Southern European Renaissance humanism: when God is deemphasized, the state is enthroned, and the individual tends to be deprived of liberty insofar as he may be out of accord with the current policy of the state. In England, Arminianism tended to go hand in hand with monarchical absolutism (Laud was Arminian). John Leith has well described the relationship: "But Arminianism was also identified with a more relaxed attitude toward theology and also toward the discipline of the Christian life. It was likewise associated with episcopacy and the divine right of kings."[60] On the contrary, in Scotland—and later in England—Calvinism was associated with the struggle for civil and religious freedom. This explains the potent dynamics that attended the signing of the Solemn League and Covenant in Scotland and then in England.

The Solemn League and Covenant bound those who took it to "the preservation of the reformed religion in the Church of Scotland . . . the reformation of religion in the kingdoms of England and Ireland in doctrine, worship, discipline, and government, according to the word of God and the example of the best reformed Churches . . . that the Churches of God in the three kingdoms might be brought to the nearest conjunction and uniformity in religion, confession of faith, form of Church government, directory for worship and catechizing." This meant that the English Parliament would be responsible for conjunction and uniformity between the church in England and in Scotland in four particulars: confession of faith, form of church government, directory for worship, and catechism. Warfield summarizes the effects of this bond: "The significance of the Solemn League and Covenant was, therefore, that it pledged the two nations to uniformity in their religious establishments and pledged them to a uniformity on the model of the establishment already existing in the Church of Scotland."[61]

Changes in the Work of the Westminster Assembly

The Solemn League and Covenant was taken by the Scottish Convention of Estates, the general assembly, and vast numbers of the people in services marked by a sense of both repentance and joy and a renewal of faith and obedience. The English Parliament and the Westminster divines (with the exception of Dr. Burgess) then subscribed the document, and sent copies of it to churches throughout the land. Multitudes willingly signed it, though some seem to have been pushed into signing it, and some—as MacCormack has shown—refused.[62] The king had already in 1642 declared both houses of Parliament guilty of high treason and, as was to be expected, issued from Oxford on 9 October 1613 a proclamation that declared the Solemn League and Covenant "a traitorous and seditious combination against us."[63] But this made little practical difference.

"By the Solemn League and Covenant, therefore, the work of the Assembly of Divines was revolutionized, and not only directed to a new end but put upon a wholly new basis."[64] The task of revising the Thirty-Nine Articles was dropped, and hereafter the Westminster Assembly was to direct its energies to carrying out the "four parts of uniformity" mentioned above. On 12 October 1643 the assembly "received an order from both Houses of Parliament, requiring them to direct their deliberations to the important topics of discipline, and a directory of worship and government."[65] It was agreed that the assembly should begin with a subject that was to prove more divisive than anything else in their deliberations: church government.

The Scottish Commissioners

The primary importance of church government and its necessary independence from the civil magistrate, in addition to much else that developed in the Westminster Assembly, were shaped by five Scottish commissioners. Even before the signing of the Solemn League and Covenant, the English Parliament had asked the appointment of Scottish delegates "to assist at" the deliberations at Westminster.[66] The general assembly of the Church of Scotland accordingly did so. These men were not merely individual members of the assembly; they had a far more influential role as a group. Carruthers explains: "That they were intended to be not merely individual assessors to the Westminster Assembly, but a body which could take corporate action, is clearly shewn by the fact that 'any three were a quorum' (Baillie, ii, 96)."[67] Warfield describes them as treaty commissioners, whose "immediate relations were not with the Assembly of Divines but with the

Parliament or with whatever commissioners the Parliament might appoint to represent it in conference with them."[68] Thus, "the proper task of the Scotch Commissioner lay not in the Assembly of Divines, but outside of it. It was their function, speaking broadly, to see that such formularies were proposed to the two contracting nations for the reducing of their church establishments to uniformity, as would be acceptable to the Church of Scotland which they represented, and would fulfill the provisions of the Solemn League and Covenant under the sanctions of which they were acting."[69]

The Scottish commissioners did have an immense influence in the deliberations of the assembly, in which they took part as individuals: "As they were requested by Parliament also 'as private men' to sit in the Assembly of Divines they occupied a sort of dual position relatively to the Assembly. . . ."[70]

Yet they clearly saw themselves first of all as treaty commissioners and in their position as intermediaries between the assembly and Parliament exercised decisive sway at various critical junctures in a way that individual members of the assembly could not have done: "Accordingly, a committee of Parliament was appointed (October 17-20, 1643) to meet statedly with them and consult with them, to which was added a committee from the Divines; and it was through this 'Grand Committee' that the work of the Assembly on the points of uniformity was directed."[71]

Hetherington gives a good description of the six Scots commissioners.[72] The lay elders, Lord Maitland and Archibald Johnston of Warriston were in regular attendance, as were the four Scottish divines: Alexander Henderson, George Gillespie, Samuel Rutherford, and Robert Baillie.

Parties in the Westminster Assembly

We have indicated that the first task given to the assembly after the signing of the Solemn League and Covenant and the arrival of the Scottish commissioners was to settle the highly disputed question of church government. This was undoubtedly the most difficult work the assembly had to face, and it spent more time debating it than any other matter, precisely because the assembly itself was divided into three parties on the question. Furthermore, the difficulty of reaching a consensus was increased by the hostility of Parliament to the majority party of the assembly on this point.

The majority party in the Westminster Assembly was by far the Presbyterians. Most of the English Puritan divines in the assembly strongly favored church government by presbytery, though some of them (Twisse, Gataker, Gouge, Palmer, Temple), like Bishop Ussher, preferred a Presbyterianism that retained some form of bishops.[73] The Scottish commissioners, though convinced Presbyterians, hoped to mediate differences that arose in the debates between probishop and antibishop Presbyterians and Independents in order to reach an amicable consensus.

The Independents were a small but able party, who "held the entire power of government to belong to each separate congregation; and they practically admitted no Church censure but admonition. . . ."[74] Knowing they could not win in open voting, the Independents "adopted an obstructive policy, and set themselves not only to obtain every concession it was possible to wring from the majority, but to delay the adoption of its scheme of Presbyterian government, and if possible, to defeat its establishment altogether."[75] The leading Independents or "five dissenting brethren" were Dr. Thomas Goodwin, Philip Nye, Jeremiah Burroughs, William Bridge, and Sidrach Simpson, plus a few others such as Carter, Caryl, Phillips, and Sterry.

The Independent desire to hinder, or better yet, abolish Presbyterian government was aided by the third and smallest party in the assembly—the Erastians:

> . . . so called from Erastus, a physician at Heidelberg, who wrote on the subject of Church government, especially in respect of excommunication, in the year 1568. His theory was,—that the pastoral office is only persuasive. . . . The punishment of all offenses . . . belonged . . . exclusively to the civil magistrate. The tendency of this theory was, to destroy entirely all ecclesiastical and spiritual jurisdiction, to deprive the Church of all power of government, and to make it completely the mere "creature of the State."[76]

There were few Erastians in the assembly, but they were exceptionally able scholars and speakers such as Lightfoot, Coleman, and Selden, as well as the lay assessors Whitelock and St. John. Their influence was out of all proportion to their insignificant numbers because their opinion was backed by the vast majority of the House of Commons, which Baillie describes as follows: "The most part of the House of Commons, especially the lawyers, whereof they are many, and divers of them very able men, are either half or whole Erastians, believing no Church-government to be of divine right, but all to be a humane constitution, depending on the will of the magistrates." (Here we may note that the Erastian polity of Richard Hooker had exercised a pervasive influence in England on the two generations of leadership between its publication and the English Civil War). Baillie also stated in 1646 that two-thirds of Parliament was made up of worldly, profane men, who would have no ecclesiastical discipline if they could avoid it, Erastians, and Erastianizing lawyers, together with a small but influential band of Independents.[77] MacCormack says the Erastian lawyers "were terrified at the thought of the minatory rule of an English version of the Kirk."[78] We can therefore see why Baillie's remark was directly to the point, that "the power of the Parliament in ecclesiastick affairs" was the greatest of the questions to be determined (2:205).[79] We must presently return to the reasons for and ramifications of the Erastianism of Parliament.

Assembly Debates on Church Government and Conflict with Parliament

It is not our purpose here to enter into the long and complex details of the various church government debates in the Westminster Assembly; this has been done very competently in the standard reference works of Mitchell, Hetherington, and Carruthers.[80] Instead, we are to focus our attention on the basic theological and political issues involved, which serve as a mirror of the intellectual, spiritual, and civil ferment of the time. The deliberations in turn became a contributory source to later thought and practice relating to civil and religious liberty, as well as to church-state relationships.

We have seen that Parliament was most interested in the subject on which the three parties of the assembly were most divided: the proper form of church government. And it was to this subject that Parliament directed the assembly to proceed after the arrival of the Scottish commissioners. The assembly determined that Scripture did in fact lay down a specific form of church government; and notwithstanding the Erastians, who following in the line of Richard Hooker denied this, the assembly then proceeded to determine of what sort it was. The majority agreed that Christ alone was Head of the church. This is reflected in chapters 8, 23, and 25 of the Westminster Confession of Faith and is the first of the propositions concerning church government, as printed in Scotland.[81] The assertion of the headship of Christ over the church, when this came to be elaborated in specific detail by the assembly, would have far-reaching civil and ecclesiastical implications of a very disturbing nature to the Erastians who controlled Parliament. The working out of these details with consequent division between the majorities of the assembly and the Parliament was not really long in coming. Yet the assembly, owing to its own internal divisions, did debate these matters for many months before a full report on ordination and on the form of church government was actually ready for presentation to Parliament.

The assembly discussed church offices in order to decide which were still valid, and which had passed away in the apostolic age.[82] Of most interest of course for presbyterians was the discussion on the nature of the eldership. (The word *presbyter* is Greek for "elder," and is the key to the Presbyterian system of representational government through elders.)[83] The findings of the assembly are summarized in this proposition, which they adopted, and which was to cause them serious problems with the Parliament: "The government which is *jure divino* [i.e., laid down in Scripture by divine law] is that which is by *preaching* and *ruling* elders in presbyteries and synods by way of subordination and appeal."[84] The Independents inside both the assembly and the Parliament were unhappy with this assertion, because they wanted the rule to rest in the local congregation rather than in the presbytery (the regional assembly of elders from the churches of that district). And the Erastians were profoundly displeased because they did not want any sort of church government to be considered binding for all time *jure divino*. Baillie, with some sarcasm, but a good deal of truth, said, "The

Pope and the King were never more earnest for the headship of the Church than the pluralitie of this Parliament."[85]

Warfield's assessment seems correct that Parliament was not opposed to Presbyterianism per se, but to *jure divino* Presbyterianism: "Parliament was in no sense averse to a Presbyterian settlement. What it was unalterably opposed to was a *jus divinum* [divine right] settlement of any kind. It was of the strongest conviction, in even its most Puritan element, that the Church derived all its authority and jurisdiction from the State; and it identified the State with itself."[86] One member of the Independent party of the assembly, Nye, threw his weight with the Erastians at this point. He undoubtedly uttered the essential critique by parliamentarian Erastianism against *jure divino* Presbyterianism "as prejudicial to the civil state, and maintained that the system of gathering into one the churches of an entire kingdom tended to encroach on the civil domain, and was thrice over pernicious to the state."[87] Thus the Parliament (or at least its Erastian majority) saw the issue at stake as a power struggle. If the church were granted autonomy over its own affairs and freedom from state control (as required by the *jure divino* position, which the Presbyterians believed to be patent in Scripture), then Parliament feared the various church judicatories (such as presbytery, synod, and general assembly) could become a rival power in the country, threatening the uniform authority of the civil government over the people. As Warfield explains: "Accordingly, when the 'Propositions concerning Church Government' came up to Parliament this was the rock on which it struck. Parliament was very willing to order the churches on the Presbyterian model, but not to erect independent judicatories, founded in a divine right, and exercising their functions uncontrolled by Parliament."[88]

The battle over state control of ecclesiastical functions ranged around a handful of important spiritual responsibilities, which Parliament felt had civil ramifications. At the center of these concerns was the matter of church discipline, and particularly the keeping back of the unworthy from the Lord's Supper. The assembly Presbyterians, following the New Testament, maintained that this was a spiritual function to be performed by spiritual officers—elders. However, ". . . when the question of the administration of the Sacrament of the

Lord's Supper and the exclusion of the scandalous from it, came up, Parliament absolutely refused to commit to the church officers in congregational or classical assemblies, the determination of what sins should be accounted scandals excluding from the Sacrament, and insisted upon itself making an enumeration of such scandals, and reserving in all other cases appeal to itself. . . . It was on this point that the sharpest conflict between Parliament and Assembly took place."[89]

Parliament was not satisfied with claiming the right to subsume the ecclesiastical function of determining who should take communion; it also insisted that the decisions of such church courts as should be set up should be liable to appeal to Parliament, thus giving Parliament ultimate control over the total life of the church. These ecclesiastical functions which Parliament was eager to take over have been summarized by Mitchell as "the scabrous questions": "of the autonomy of the Church, the supremacy of its Divine Head, and the independence of its officers in the administration of the discipline of His house,—questions which divided the friends of the Reformation in the Assembly and in the Parliament . . . seriously . . . and the differences . . . were one main cause why Presbyterianism was never fully set up in England."[90] We must consider why Parliament wanted to lay claim to these high powers and why the assembly felt it essential to stand firm against these claims at all costs.

It has already been indicated that Parliament feared an autonomous church free from state control as a rival power in the life of the nation. But why should a largely Puritan Parliament have held this viewpoint? Rosenstock-Huessy traces this attitude to the historical English experience that led to the effective replacement of monarchical power by parliamentary power (which was not reversed even by the 1660 restoration of King Charles II).[91]

Perhaps even more to the point in explaining the increasing parliamentary coolness towards a true Presbyterian church settlement on the Scottish model (which is what Parliament after all had suggested in their original ordinance calling the Westminster Assembly and even more specifically in the Solemn League and Covenant, which they adopted) was the lack of English historical precedence for a nationally functioning Presbyterian system. Hill has traced the widespread seventeenth-century Independency among English Puritans to destruction by Elizabeth I's High Commission of the Presbyterian Classical Movement in the 1580s and 1590s, so that while Puritanism continued, a functioning Presbyterian system was never able to develop in England.[92] Though the cases were very different indeed, there is at least some analogy between the Scottish revolt against the foreign intrusion of bishops, and the English rejection of (as far as national English historical precedent is concerned) "foreign" presbytery, synod, and general assembly.

To this factor must be added the widespread influence of the theories of the judicious Hooker, who held that church government is not specifically defined by Scripture for all times and places, but may be adjusted to the historical context in accordance with basic natural law as interpreted by the civil magistrate, who thus has the final say, as we have seen earlier. Such theories were only too welcomed by a Parliament that had ridded itself of a powerful monarch, and now, jealous of its power, had every motivation to keep a strong church from developing.

Indeed, Parliament did not merely attempt to keep the state-church balance as it was; it actually assumed innovative (and to that degree revolutionary) powers over the church. Dr. Shaw has described this as "the unscrupulous and revolutionary seizure by the Parliament of every part of the domain of ecclesiastical jurisdiction which had hitherto in whole or part belonged peculiarly to the spiritual courts" (*A History of the English Church During . . . 1640-1660*, (1900), 1:227 sqq.).[93] The Reformed or Calvinist balance between nature and grace and the consequent balance between church and individual on the one hand and proper state order on the other never took hold so completely in England (even during the Puritan triumph) as it did in Scotland.

For their part, the Presbyterian majority of the Westminster Assembly believed that in standing for the liberties of the church against state control, they were contending for "the Crown rights of Jesus Christ," and that he alone and not any earthly Parliament was "the only Law giver in Zion." They also believed that if the state could control the church and thus suppress Christian liberties, there would be nothing to stop it from going on to suppress civil liberties as well. Hence religious liberty was seen as a mainstay of personal civil liberties. A great deal more, therefore, was involved in these arguments than merely ecclesiastical concerns, though ecclesiastical concerns were paramount—especially since the assembly majority felt the whole matter turned on the lordship of Christ.

The Scottish commissioners were of great influence in encouraging the assembly to stand for church liberty as an expression of the lordship of Christ against both Erastians and Independents within the assembly and against the powerful Erastian majority of Parliament. An illustration of the Scottish stand for church autonomy from state control within the assembly is the famous argument between the young and brilliant Scots divine, Gillespie, and the distinguished oriental scholar, Selden, who was a strong Erastian.[94]

In what was an even more difficult situation, the Scots commissioner Sir Archibald Johnston, a lay elder, defended the principles of Christian liberty in a very effective speech, not only before the assembly, but also before a committee from the Parliament, which was considering legal action against the assembly for its refusal to accept the advice of Parliament on the controverted matter of state control over the church:

> . . . Christ's throne is highest, and his privilege supreme as only head and king of his Church, albeit kings and magistrates may be members in it. There is no authority to be balanced with his, nor post to be set up against his post. . . . Is it so small a thing to have the sword that they must have the keys also. . . ?[95]

Both Erastian Parliament and libertarian Presbyterian assembly saw this question as one of utmost historical importance, as evidenced by the serious conflict that developed between them, to which Sir Archibald Johnston's speech was a reaction. Without reviewing all the details of this controversy, which has been elucidated by Mitchell, we may note that the assembly protested certain changes made by the House of Commons in the assembly report concerning the church's duty and right to exclude the scandalous from the Lord's Supper.[96] The assembly essentially refused to allow these Erastianizing changes on the grounds of their commitment to scriptural teaching and to the lordship of Christ, a refusal Parliament took as an impertinent challenge of its authority.

In a technical sense, Parliament still had the last word, for "The final Ordinance of Parliament on church-government, embodying and supplementing or making permanent the former ones, still contained the clause authorizing appeals from the Church courts to Parliament. . . ."[97] Mitchell, Hetherington, and MacCormack have all demonstrated that Parliament tended to take a more arrogant attitude towards the Westminster Assembly precisely at those times when the parliamentary military forces were having greater success against the king, and thus the need of Scottish military aid was felt less strongly.[98] MacCormack also demonstrates an alliance between the Presbyterian majority of the assembly and the generally pro-Presbyterian "moderate" party of the House of Commons.[99] The Scottish commissioners, as well as many others in the assembly and the moderates in the house, opposed to absolute monarchy, were also opposed to what they saw as parliamentarian Erastian tyranny. They favored a constitutional, limited monarchy and thus were opposed to a radical commonwealth. However, the "radical" party of the House of Commons gained the upper hand, and they favored elimination of the monarchy, Erastian control of the church, and the establishment of a commonwealth. As this party grew stronger, it behaved in a more antagonistic way toward the assembly; for it perceived the assembly to stand between it and the strong statist power it wished to assume in the name of the people.

Articles of Faith

Unlike the hostile atmosphere that prevailed at times between the assembly and Parliament, and indeed between the differing parties within the assembly while the form of church government was being debated, the several months spent on compiling and perfecting the confession of faith were characterized in general by harmony and amicable cooperation. In the words of Hetherington:

> . . . when composing the Confession of Faith, there prevailed almost an entire and perfect harmony. There appear, indeed, to have been only two subjects on which any difference of opinion existed among them. The one of these was the doctrine of election, concerning which, as Baillie says, they had long and tough debates; "Yet," he

> adds,"thanks to God, all is gone right according to our mind." The other was . . . that "the Lord Jesus, as King and Head of His Church, has therein appointed a government in the hand of Church-officers distinct from the civil magistrate;" which appears as the fundamental proposition of the chapter entitled "Of Church censures." This proposition the Assembly manifestly intended and understood to contain a principle directly and necessarily opposed to the very essence of Erastianism . . . consequently it became the subject of long and earnest discussion. . . . Some discussion took place on the thirty-first chapter in the Confession, respecting Synods and Councils; but that subject also was carried in the express language of the Assembly, and without any Erastian modification.[100]

The English Parliament did not approve the confession until the summer of 1648 and ordered it to be published in London with a changed title: "Articles of Christian religion approved and passed by both Houses of Parliament after advice had with the Assembly of Divines." Mitchell explains that "this title was adopted because it was in nearer agreement with that of the Thirty-nine Articles, and also because the treatise was not in the direct form of a Confession, i.e. with the words 'I confess,' 'We confess'. . . ."[101]

Parliament made some final changes in the confession, most of which related to their Erastianism, as Dr. Leith explains:

> The version that was ordered printed by the House of Commons on June 20, 1648, omits Chapter XXX, "Of Church Censures," and Chapter XXXI, "Of Synods and Councils." It also omits the fourth paragraph of chapter 20, which related Christian liberty to the power of the civil magistrate, and part of the fourth paragraph and all of the fifth and sixth paragraphs of chapter 24 that have to do with marriage. While Parliament shared the basic theological convictions of the confession, it is apparent there was no consensus as to the nature of the church or as to the interrelationship of church and society.[102]

Undoubtedly of more significance for later church history was the approval of the original confession of faith (under this first title, and without the English parliamentary changes) by the general assembly of the Church of Scotland in 1647, "after specifying its own interpretation of Chapter XXXI, paragraph 3, that gave the state the right to call synods. The General Assembly said this would hold only in the case of churches that were not settled or constituted. The Parliament of Scotland ratified it in 1649."[103]

> In 1654 there was a movement in Cromwell's first Parliament for the calling of a new assembly and the writing of another statement of faith. This came to naught. In 1660 the reassembled Rump Parliament adopted the Confession of the Westminster Assembly with the exception of Chapters XXX and XXXI. This concluded the work that began with hope and expectancy in 1642 and 1643.[104]

Parliament did not succeed in establishing a respected, popularly based civil government, so that it was ripe for the takeover by Oliver Cromwell and for the Commonwealth or interregnum period, between the purge of Parliament in 1648 and the restoration of the king in 1660. Even with the lack of appropriate forms of limited and constitutional civil government, still the Long Parliament and Cromwell did much of benefit for England—and for the world.[105]

Cromwell died in 1658 and was succeeded by his son, Richard, a worthy person by all accounts, but not able to exercise the leadership essential to the position. In the words of Christopher Hill, "Richard Cromwell lacked the prestige with soldiers necessary if he was to prolong his father's balancing trick but after his fall no Army leader proved capable of restoring the old radical alliance, and nothing but social revolution could have thwarted the 'natural rulers' determination to get rid of military rule."[106]

At the same time, events in Europe made many in England and Scotland believe that restoration of the king would be the safest policy for national defense:

> The foreign situation helped to make Charles' restoration technically unconditional: there was a general fear that the peace of November 1659 which ended 24 years of war between France and Spain would be followed by an alliance of the two countries to restore the Stuarts. Once it seemed likely that Charles would return, most of those who had fought against his father hastened to show their loyalty to the son.[107]

With the restoration of the king came very soon afterwards the restoration of Anglicanism with its bishops and *via media* position. That position, with the prominence it gave to nature and man's reasoning, made it far more open than Calvinism to the resurgence of humanist thought now abroad in Europe. At first the Presbyterians and Puritans had hoped for amicable compromise. But as Elniff states, "In England Presbyterians joined with Anglicans to restore Charles II to the throne in 1660, shortly after which the Anglicans turned on the Presbyterians and expelled them from the Church of England."[108]

The restoration brought in a period of strong reaction against Puritanism and Calvinism both theologically and morally. Hill says, "Godliness was at a discount at the court of the merry monarch, but the cult of King Charles the martyr prospered."[109] That is to say, as anti-Puritanism in theology and morals increased, the theology and practice of divine right kingship and centralized statist control also increased. The English reaction against the Calvinists' belief in two concurrent kingdoms—church and state with consequent separation, limitation, and balance of powers under the critical guidance of transcendent law—and their turning back to an essentially one-kingdom, one-power theory was not an isolated event in late seventeenth-century Europe. It was part of the intellectual climate of that time, which was preparing the way for the eighteenth-century Enlightenment. That was to be a move away from both Calvinism and traditional Roman Catholicism.

Soon after the restoration of the monarchy, Charles II began systematically prosecuting all who would not "conform" to the reestablished Episcopal system of the traditional Anglican Church. By 1662, in a series of parliamentary measures known as the Clarendon Acts, the rights of the formerly triumphant non-Anglicans such as Presbyterians, Congregationalists, Baptists, and Quakers (not to mention the still suppressed Roman Catholics) to hold religious assemblies, preach, teach, and proselytize were removed. Hundreds of pro-Puritan and pro-Presbyterian clergymen were officially ejected from the regnant Anglican establishment.

We have already seen how restoration of Episcopacy in Scotland led to widespread defiance and consequent persecution of the Covenanters. So also in Britain, Presbyterian forms of Calvinism seemed to have lost any significant political influence. Yet "the English Revolution" was not over.

Without treating details, we may briefly note that Charles II died without legitimate offspring and was succeeded by his brother James II (VII of Scotland). He declared openly his Roman Catholicism and intent to force the nation to forsake Anglicanism in order to reconform to Catholicism. He had seriously misread the mind of the nation. Once again covenantal arguments that clearly owed something to Calvinism—this time used not by French Huguenots or Scottish Covenanters or even significantly by English Puritans, but by British Anglicans—were brought forward to justify deposing King James and replacing him with his Protestant daughter, Mary, and her husband, William of Orange.

James was said to have broken the terms of agreement by which he had ascended the throne.[110] Undoubtedly the framework, as well as details of this "Whig" justification for removing the Catholic monarch was much more directly based on late sixteenth- and seventeenth-century natural law reasoning—especially as this was mediated through the crucial writings of John Locke—than on Calvinist religious sources. Yet the basic concept used to justify James's removal was covenantally based, indirectly harking back to both Catholic conciliarism and Calvinist constitutionalism. The details were worked out more directly in terms of popular sovereignty and natural rights than, let us say, in terms of Knoxian religious mandate to uproot idolatry. The French Huguenots had already pointed in this direction, as had Buchanan, Althusius, and to a certain degree Samuel Rutherford.[111]

Yet the English Puritan experience had more lingering influence than merely supplying part of the framework of thought for deposing the "tyrant." From this time on—after 1688—the power of absolute monarchy in England was severely limited. Although by no means an exclusively or even originally Calvinist concept, limitation of governmental powers generally tended to exist where Calvinist influence had been strong. This was still the case in many respects in late seventeenth-century England. And though other important intellectual factors—particularly early "Enlightenment" natural law thinking—entered into the equation, the final limitation of monarchical power in England owed to the Calvinist antecedents.

If we may properly think of Calvinism as influencing England in the matter of limitation of monarchical power, we must at the same time recognize that unlike more thoroughly Calvinist Scotland, the Calvinist concept of division and balance of powers did not prevail in the same way in England even after 1688. As Rosenstock-Huessy has pointed out, the king's absolute power was basically transferred to Parliament (albeit in the name of the people).[112] And as Lyall has stated, "the theory of the single sovereign from whom all power is drawn, expressed in Hobbes' *Leviathan* and later in the theory of John Austin" was to become predominant.[113] Thus the Westminster Assembly's profoundly Calvinist desire to have a two-kingdoms, two-powers view and practice of church-state relations failed. And England's "restoration" position on the relation of civil and ecclesiastical powers in a sense owed more to the Henrician settlement than to Calvin's successors at the Westminster Assembly.

Nonetheless, there were profound differences between the settlements of the 1530s and the 1680s, and these differences owed a great deal to the Puritan struggle. There was now relative toleration of non-Anglicans in England and restoration of Presbyterianism in Scotland. Perhaps more importantly, there was a common stock of concepts dealing with religious and civil relationships and rights that had strong Calvinist affinities as well as natural law ancestry. Increasingly, politicians had to take these popular concepts into consideration in order to maintain their power.

If the influence of Calvinism in postrevolutionary England was rather limited, it would be considerably greater in prerevolutionary America.

Notes

[1] Quentin Skinner, *The Foundations of Modern Political Thought* (Cambridge: Cambridge University Press, 1978), 2:60.

[2] Owen Chadwick, *The Reformation* (Baltimore: Penguin Books, 1964), p. 22.

[3] W. M. Hetherington (Robert Williamson, ed.), *History of the Westminster Assembly of Divines*, 4th ed. (Edinburgh: James Gemmell, 1878), p. 23.

[4] Chadwick, *The Reformation*, p. 101.

[5] Ibid., p. 115.

[6] Ibid., p. 117.

[7] Ibid., p. 123.

[8] Ibid., p. 128.

[9] Ibid., p. 212.

[10] R. T. Kendall questions its usefulness in *Calvin and English Calvinism to 1649* (Oxford: Oxford University Press, 1981), p. 5.

[11] Christopher Hill, *Society and Puritanism* (New York: Schocken Books, 1964, 1967), chapter 1.

[12] Ibid., pp. 28, 29.

[13] Christopher Hill, *Intellectual Origins of the English Revolution* (Oxford: Oxford University Press, 1965), p. 293.

[14] Chadwick, *The Reformation*, p. 214.

[15] Alexander F. Mitchell, *The Westminster Assembly: Its History and Standards*, 2nd ed. (Philadelphia: Presbyterian Board of Publication, 1897), pp. 3, 4, 5.

[16] Hetherington, *History of the Westminster Assembly*, p. 21.

[17] Mitchell, *Westminster Assembly*, p. 5.

[18] Douglas F. Kelly, "Richard Hooker," in *Evangelical Dictionary of Theology* (Grand Rapids: Baker, 1984), pp. 531-32.

[19] Iain Murray, *The Puritan Hope* (London: Banner of Truth, 1971), p. 4.

[20] Ibid., p. 3.

[21] Christopher Hill, *Puritanism and Revolution* (New York: Schocken Books, 1958, 1970), p. 23.

[22] Chaps. 1 and 6 of Hill's *Puritanism and Revolution* give illuminating interpretations of this matter.

[23] Hill, *Society and Puritanism*, p. 27.

[24] See Hill's *Puritanism and Revolution*, chaps. 1, 4, 6, 10 for an excellent survey of English Civil War terminology and interpretations.

[25] Christopher Hill, *God's Englishman: Oliver Cromwell and the English Revolution* (New York: Harper and Row, 1970, 1972), p. 13.

[26] Ibid., p. 250.

[27] Hill, *Puritanism and Revolution*, pp. 46, 47.

[28] Hill, *Society and Puritanism*, p. 40.

[29] Ibid., pp. 345, 348.

[30] Ibid., p. 348.

[31] Hill, *Intellectual Origins*, p. 256.

[32] See C. Hill on "The Norman Yoke" (chap. 3) in *Puritanism and Revolution*, and on "Sir Edward Coke—Myth-maker" (chap. 5) in *Intellectual Origins*.

[33] Eugen Rosenstock-Huessy, *Out of Revolution* (Norwich, Vt.: Argo Books, 1969), p. 270, 278.

[34] See Hetherington, *History of the Westminster Assembly*, p. 55; Mitchell, *Westminster Assembly*, pp. 351-52; and Rosenstock-Huessy, *Out of Revolution*, pp. 272-77.

[35] Mitchell, *Westminster Assembly*, p. 69.

[36] Ibid., p. 70.

[37] Ibid., p. 72.

[38] Ibid., pp. 84, 85.

[39] Ibid., p. 86.

[40] Donald MacLean, *Aspects of Scottish Church History* (Edinburgh: T. & T. Clark, 1927), p. 47.

[41] Ibid., p. 92.

[42] Hetherington, *History of the Westminster Assembly*, pp. 68, 69.

[43] J. H. S. Burleigh, *A Church History of Scotland* (London: Oxford University Press, 1960, 1961), p. 222.

[44] Ibid., pp. 222, 223.

[45] John R. MacCormack, *Revolutionary Politics in the Long Parliament* (Cambridge, Mass.: Harvard University Press, 1973), pp. 8-10.

[46] Hetherington, *History of the Westminster Assembly*, p. 74.

[47] Ibid., p. 76.

[48] Ibid., p. 88.

[49] Rosenstock-Huessy, *Out of Revolution*, p. 308.

[50] Robert Baillie, *The Letters and Journals of Robert Baillie 1637-1662*, ed. David Laing, 3 vols. (Edinburgh: Robert Ogle, 1841), 2:186, quoted in S. W. Carruthers, *The Everyday Work of the Westminster Assembly* (Philadelphia: The Presbyterian Historical Society of America and of England, 1943), p. 5.

[51] Hetherington, *History of the Westminster Assembly*, p. 108.

[52] Carruthers, *Work of the Westminster Assembly*, p. 13.

[53] Benjamin B. Warfield, *The Westminster Assembly and Its Work* (Cherry Hill, N.J.: Mack, 1972), p. 23 n. 38, citing J. A. R. Marriott, *The Life and Times of Lucius Cary* (Viscount Falkland, 1907), p. 303.

[54] Warfield, *Westminster Assembly and Its Work*, pp. 22, 23.

[55] Baillie, *Letters and Journals*, p. 90.

[56] Warfield, *Westminster Assembly and Its Work*, p. 23.

[57] Hetherington, *History of the Westminster Assembly*, p. 117.

[58] See *The Covenants and the Covenanters*, comp. James Kerr (Edinburgh: R. W. Hunter, George IV Bridge, 1895), pp. 131-35.

[59] So named for the Dutch "Remonstrant" theologian, Jacobus Arminius, who originally studied under Calvin's successor at Geneva, Theodore Beza. The "Remonstrants" represented a liberalizing trend in European theological thought, which deemphasized the sovereignty of God in salvation in the interest of emphasizing man's participation and importance in it. The "five points of Calvinism" formulated at the Synod of Dort in 1618-19 (total depravity of man, unconditional election, limited atonement, irresistible grace, and perseverance of the saints) were the Calvinist response to the five liberalizing theses of the Arminians.

[60] John H. Leith, *Assembly at Westminster: Reformed Theology in the Making* (Richmond, Va.: John Knox Press, 1973), p. 26.

[61] Warfield, *Westminster Assembly and Its Work*, p. 26.

[62] MacCormack, *Revolutionary Politics*, pp. 11-13. See also Carruthers, *Work of the Westminster Assembly*, pp. 18-21.

[63] Hetherington, *History of the Westminster Assembly*, p. 121.

[64] Warfield, *Westminster Assembly and Its Work*, p. 34.

[65] Hetherington, *History of the Westminster Assembly*, p. 152.

[66] Eight commissioners (four clergy, four lay elders) were originally chosen "and were fairly representative of the Church of Scotland, in the two parties into which it was then divided with respect to its sympathies with the old order in Scotland or with 'the movement party in the South,' that is, the Puritans. Robert Douglas, Alexander Henderson, Robert Baillie, with the Earl of Cassilis and Lord Maitland, belonged to one side; Samuel Rutherford, George Gillespie, and Archibald Johnston of Warriston to the other. . . . Douglas and Cassilis never went up to London. . . " (Warfield, *Westminster Assembly and Its Work*, p. 30 n. 58).

[67] Carruthers, *Work of the Westminster Assembly*, p. 23.

[68] Warfield, *Westminster Assembly and Its Work*, p. 32.

[69] Ibid., pp. 31, 32.

[70] Ibid., p. 33.

[71] Ibid.

[72] Hetherington, *History of the Westminster Assembly*, pp. 139-42.

[73] Warfield, *Westminster Assembly and Its Work*, p. 37.

[74] Hetherington, *History of the Westminster Assembly*, p. 131.

[75] Warfield, *Westminster Assembly and Its Work*, p. 37.

[76] Hetherington, *History of the Westminster Assembly*, p. 134.

[77] Warfield, *Westminster Assembly and Its Work*, pp. 37, 38 n. 72.

[78] MacCormack, *Revolutionary Politics*, p. 110.

[79] Warfield, *Westminster Assembly and Its Work*, p. 38 n. 72.

[80] See Mitchell, *Westminster Assembly*, Lectures 6-9; Hetherington, *History of the Westminster Assembly*, chaps. 4-7; Carruthers, *Work of the Westminster Assembly*, chap. 2.

[81] Mitchell, *Westminster Assembly*, p. 188.

[82] See Hetherington, *History of the Westminster Assembly*, pp. 154-58, for details.

[83] See Mitchell, *Westminster Assembly*, pp. 192-94, for details.

[84] Ibid., p. 196.

[85] Baillie, *Letters and Journals*, p. 360.

[86] Warfield, *Westminster Assembly and Its Work*, p. 40 n. 78.

[87] Mitchell, *Westminster Assembly*, p. 201.

[88] Warfield, *Westminster Assembly and Its Work*, pp. 40-41 n. 78.

[89] Ibid.

[90] Mitchell, *Westminster Assembly*, p. 278.

[91] Rosenstock-Huessy, *Out of Revolution*, pp. 317-18.

[92] Christopher Hill, *Society and Puritanism*, pp. 502, 503.

[93] Quoted in Warfield, *Westminster Assembly and Its Work*, p. 41 n. 79.

[94] For details of these debates, see Hetherington, *History of the Westminster*

Assembly, pp. 235-40.

[95] Mitchell, *Westminster Assembly*, pp. 325-27.

[96] See ibid., pp. 301-34, for details.

[97] Ibid., p. 330.

[98] See ibid., p. 205; Hetherington, *History of the Westminster Assembly*, pp. 258, 272; MacCormack, *Revolutionary Politics*, pp. 41, 95.

[99] See MacCormack, *Revolutionary Politics*, pp. 32-91.

[100] Hetherington, *History of the Westminster Assembly*, pp. 285, 286.

[101] Mitchell, *Westminster Assembly*, p. 379.

[102] Leith, *Assembly at Westminster*, p. 62.

[103] Ibid., p. 63.

[104] Ibid., p. 62.

[105] See Christopher Hill's biography, *God's Englishman*.

[106] Ibid., p. 253.

[107] Ibid.

[108] Terrill Elniff, *The Guise of Every Graceless Heart: Human Autonomy in Puritan Thought and Experience* (Vallecito, Calif.: Ross House Books, 1981), p. 79.

[109] Hill, *God's Englishman*, p. 253.

[110] Cf. Francis Lyall, *Of Presbyters and Kings: Church and State in the Law of Scotland* (Aberdeen: Aberdeen University Press, 1980), p. 19.

[111] Though Thomas Carlyle in his typical nineteenth-century essayist style overstates the case, he does make a valid point on this matter: "The Puritanism of Scotland became that of England, of New England. A tumult in the High Church of Edinburgh spread into a universal battle and struggle over all these realms;—there came out, after fifty-years struggling, what we call the 'Glorious Revolution,' a *Habeas Corpus Act*, Free Parliaments, and much else! Alas, is it not too true what we said, That many men in the van do always, like Russian soldiers march into the ditch of Schweidniz, and fill it up with their dead bodies, that the rear may pass-over them dry-shod, and gain the honor? How many earnest rugged Cromwells, Knoxes, poor Peasant Covenanters, wrestling, battling for very life, in rough miry places, have to struggle, and suffer, and fall, greatly censured *bemired* before a beautiful Revolution of Eighty-eight can step-over them in official pumps and silk-stockings, with universal three-times-three" (Thomas Carlyle, *On Heroes, Hero-Worship and the Heroic in History* [London: Chapman and Hall, Ltd., 1872, 1897], pp. 134, 135).

[112] Rosenstock-Huessy, *Out of Revolution*, pp. 314, 315.

[113] Lyall, *Of Presbyters and Kings*, p. 22.

5

Calvinism and Government in the American Colonies

THE PURITAN MOVEMENT, which suffered political and military failure in England by 1660, exercised widespread influence in the American colonies through large immigrations of English Puritans and later "Scotch-Irish" (or "Ulster Scots") and Scots Highland Presbyterians. These people did not leave their theology behind, but rather brought with them strong views on God, man, and society in general and on church-state relations and individual civil and religious liberty in particular. Over the next six or seven generations, these Calvinist-based ideas would be worked out in various church and civil polity experiments and then would be combined with a variety of other (in the later period, secular) theories of government and liberty to give rise to the movement leading to the American War of Independence and to shape its constitutional settlement.

Puritan Revivals and American History

Chard Powers Smith, in *Yankees and God*, viewed American history as successive (and ultimately waning) waves of Puritan revivals as follows: 1630-60, then a "recession"; 1700-1760, then another recession; 1800-1860 and a recession; and finally 1900-1930, followed by another decline of Puritan faith and cultural influence.[1] Sydney Ahlstrom has suggested that "the Puritan era" in the Anglo-Saxon world lasted from the accession of Elizabeth I in 1558 to the election of John F. Kennedy as president in 1960. John Leith has wondered if Ahlstrom's conclusion of the Puritan era at 1960 may not have been premature.[2] Perry Miller wrote several now famous volumes chronicling the vast influence of Puritanism on the American culture and legal tradition.[3]

In terms of population alone, a high percentage of the prerevolutionary American colonies were of Puritan-Calvinist background. There were around three million persons in the thirteen original colonies by 1776, and perhaps as many as two-thirds of these came from some kind of Calvinist or Puritan connection. Most of seventeenth- and eighteenth-century New England had Puritan congregationalist antecedents. Although Anglicans predominated in Tidewater Virginia and Low Country South Carolina, there were Puritan sympathies among many of these Anglicans. (Sir Edwin Sandys of the Virginia Company and son of Archbishop Sandys of York had Puritan leanings.) But as far as more militant Calvinism is concerned, the greatest influence in the middle and southern colonies came from the "Scotch-Irish" ("Ulster Scots" as they are generally called in Northern Ireland), as well as from smaller numbers of Highland Scots (especially in North and South Carolina).

According to E. T. Thompson:

> Charles A. Hannah estimates that about 200,000 Protestants, most of them Presbyterians, one-third of the entire Protestant population of Ireland, left the Emerald Isle during the disastrous period 1725-1768. . . . Another thirty thousand came during the years 1771-1773. When the Revolution broke out, there were approximately 500,000 "Scotch-Irish" in America, one-sixth of the total population.[4]

These people filled up the "Piedmont" section of the Eastern Atlantic states—the interior hilly country from Pennsylvania down through the Valley of Virginia, the Carolinas, Georgia, and later into what became Alabama and Mississippi. "No other one people of uniform race, custom, religion, and political principles had made such extensive settlements in so many of the thirteen colonies."[5] Their experience of Presbyterian polity—with its doctrine of the headship of Christ over the church, the two-powers doctrine giving church and state equal standing (so that the church's power is not seen as flowing from the state), and the consequent right of the people to civil resistance in accordance with higher divine law—was a major ingredient in the development of the American approach to church-state relations and the underlying questions of law, authority, order, and rights.

Local and Colonial Government

The earliest Calvinists in America however were not the Presbyterian Scots and Scotch-Irish of the middle and southern colonies. They were preceded almost a century earlier by the Congregationalist Calvinists (or Puritans) of New England. Tens of thousands of Puritans fled from England during the persecutions against them by Archbishop Laud in the 1630s and 1640s. They continued coming even during the Commonwealth period, and their numbers increased after the restoration of the anti-Puritan monarchy in 1660. It was largely from the Congregational polity of these New England Puritans that there came the American concept and practice of government by covenant—that is to say: constitutional structure, limited by divine law and based on the consent of the people, with a lasting right in the people to resist tyranny.

The New England Congregationalists had the custom of founding each congregation upon a covenant drawn up by the local church leaders and pledged by the membership. This was a significantly different approach from the Scotch-Irish and Scots Presbyterians of the lower colonies, who organized congregations under the authority of the regional presbytery, which required subscription by the local church officers to the already written Westminster Confession of Faith. As Leonard Trinterud stated, this difference in polity between Congregationalists and Presbyterians (who were almost totally united in theology) was to lead to serious difficulties among them after their partial merger in the Plan of Union of 1801.[6] For our purposes, we may note that the constitutional experience of church covenants had a direct effect upon the development of charters (and eventually constitutions) for community and colony, and ultimately for the nation. The rather different Presbyterian polity was to contribute in its own way to later state and national practice of government by representation, checks and balances. It may well have influenced to a certain degree the courts of judicial appeal.

Under the various colonial charters, such as the Letters Patent to Sir Humphrey Gilbert (1578), the "American" colonists were required to "pledge loyalty to the crown," but were given much liberty to organize the details of their own local government, "as long as local law was not contrary to the laws of England."[7] This allowed the Puritan settlers to draw up their own civil compacts in close analogy to their church covenants. The Mayflower Compact of 11 November 1620 is an example of a Christian civil covenant creating "a civil body politic" for "the Advancement of the Christian Faith and the honor of our king and country." As Donald Lutz states, "As a complete foundational, political document, it lacks only one more element—the description of specific instructions for collective decision making, the framework of government."[8]

This necessary element for a full civil constitution was soon provided in the 1636 "Pilgrim Code of Law," which specifically described the political institutions by which they would be governed. This Pilgrim Code stated that the colonists had the same rights as all Englishmen, including the right to base government upon the consent of the governed.[9] The Fundamental Orders of Connecticut (1639) was a similar civil constitution patterned on the Calvinist Congregational church government. By 1645, "political communities from Maine to Delaware" had drawn up similar constitutions. Although these colonies were not "in close contact with each other," Lutz explains why they produced such similar documents:

> . . . their points of commonality lay in 1) a similarly desperate situation in the New World wilderness, 2) a distant mother country from which they brought the rights and political inclinations of free Englishmen, but from which they could draw no immediate succor, and 3) the bible, a close reading of which had provided them with a political technology for establishing communities. In less than two

> decades these isolated communities put this technology to similar uses and evolved an historically important idea—the written constitution found in a single document, and adopted by the citizens through their direct consent.[10]

Lutz has pointed out that the later American constitutional settlement was based on concepts from both the colonial charter (which granted power to the people from "the top down") and the colonial civil covenant (or "compact") in which the people grant political power to governmental officials "from the bottom up."[11] Similarly, Trinterud noted the contrast between Scottish Presbyterianism and its offspring in America. In Scotland, historically organizational power flowed from "the top down" in that the general assembly of the Church of Scotland was first legally established in 1560, and it then proceeded (with parliamentary approval) to establish lower synods and presbyteries (i.e., larger and smaller regional governing bodies, with rights of appeal from the smaller to the larger). But in the American colonies, local congregations and lower regional presbyteries were first established (in particular, the Presbytery of Philadelphia in 1706) and only later did the "lower" power set up synods (the Synod of Philadelphia in 1729) and general assembly (1788). Thus, in American colonial Presbyterianism (as in New England Congregational compacts), power flowed "from the bottom up" rather than from the "top down."[12] This concept of power flowing upwards rather than downwards was to have immense influence in the development of the American mind, both in its religious and civil aspects.

The idea of the colonial charter, which grants power (from London), and the Puritan congregationalist civil covenant (allowed by the original charter), by which the people specify how they are to be ruled and thus grant power to their own officials, are combined in the colonial constitutional traditional of the Eastern Atlantic Seaboard, which Lutz terms "an American hybrid":

> . . . the constitutional tradition that draws upon the legalistic, limited government, contractual aspects of the charter background and the communitarian, majoritarian, popular consent aspects of the covenant-compact background.[13]

The same writer properly points out that this "American hybrid" is derived neither from English common law nor from seventeenth-century natural law writers, nor from the eighteenth-century Enlightenment.

> In 1641, John Locke was only nine years old and Montesquieu, Rousseau, Blackstone and the other major writers prominent in late eighteenth century were not to be born for at least another half century. Yet by 1641, much of what will become American constitutional government is already operating under the early foundational documents.[14]

The origin was closer at hand: Calvinist ideas of church polity and civil liberty under transcendent law combined with the political reality of relatively generous British granted charters. The perceptive French sociologist, de Tocqueville, who visited the young American republic in the early 1830s, saw this connection between the colonial charters and civil constitutions and the underlying religious convictions. He spoke of the forward-looking principles of these documents, "which documents, though they were written two hundred years ago, are still in advance of the liberties of our age."[15] After quoting from the charters of Connecticut, Massachusetts, and others, he wrote: "The reader will undoubtedly have remarked . . . the preamble of these enactments: in America, religion is the road to knowledge, and the observance of the divine law leads men to civil freedom."[16]

After the restoration of Charles II in 1660, there was periodically discussion in London (and uneasiness in New England) over the possible loss of local governmental rights through the unilateral revocation or serious amendment of these charters by the crown. Some changes were made as "England attempted to reduce local colonial government through more restrictive royal charters. . . ."[17] But these changes did not significantly alter colonial constitutional self-government.[18]

> In fact, three of these "ratifying" types of charters (Connecticut—1662, Rhode Island—1663, and Massachusetts—1692) would in 1776 be seen as true constitutions, when, with minor amendment, they served as constitutions for these new states.[19]

Yet the continuing fear of replacement or subversion of these Calvinist-inspired charters would be a potent irritant to relations between the colonies and the British government, and a major factor leading to the War of Independence in 1776. Bridenbaugh traces this controversy during the prerevolutionary decades.[20] Their devotion to these charters was well expressed in 1765 by Dennys DeBerdt, the agent of the New England Congregationalists in London, to Lord Dartmouth, new president of the board of trade:

> Yet oppression was so much the taste of those times, that it drove out a number of the King's subjects, who took shelter in a Desart that they might enjoy their Civil and Religious Libertys, uncontroul'd and unmolested: they were then in a state of nature, under no civil government but what they form'd themselves, when they had establish'd their several Settlements, out of regard to their mother country they sent home their several agents to tender their new acquisitions to their mother country, on certain conditions then agreed on by the several parties; and ratified by their respective Charters, which they look'd on as sacred; and make boast of like our Magna Charta of England.[21]

Holy Commonwealth and Great Awakening

The attitude out of which came the colonial civil compacts was part of a broader theological, political vision held by many of the leading New England Puritan settlers—that of the American settlement or "plantation" as "a Holy Commonwealth." This itself was part of the British Puritan desire to reform the entire world. Quoting Professor Haller, Christopher Hill captured the Puritan reforming spirit:

> "Men" he adds, "who have assurance that they are to inherit heaven, have a way of presently taking possession of the earth." This courage and confidence enabled them to fight, with economic, political or military weapons, to create a new world worthy of the God who had so signally blessed them. . . .[22]

Hill adds, "Previous theologians had explained the world: for the Puritans the point was to change it."[23] And Michael Walzer quotes a

Puritan sermon before the House of Commons in 1641: "Reformation must be universal. Reform all places, all persons and callings. . . . Every plant which my heavenly Father hath not planted shall be rooted up."[24] In a chapter entitled "The Holy Commonwealth," Rushdoony summarizes the New England Puritan vision as:

> . . . not individualism but a sense of destiny as *God's chosen people*, in faith in their calling, not only in terms of the personal covenant of grace, and as a church covenant and the development of the Reformation, but as a *civil covenant*, a called people of God as a civil order, surrounded by the notable and marvelous tokens of His providence. Timothy Dwight's *Conquest of Canaan* (1785) is eloquent evidence of this faith. . . . Dwight, in "Good Advice in Bad Verse" (1787) saw the restoration of Eden as part of America's destiny and summoned America to "perfect her federal system . . . for this stupendous realm, this chosen race."[25]

Hence, unlike modern liberal democratic ideas, the New England Puritans were not primarily individualists seeking a neutral republic open to all religious views. Rather, they held to a Christian commonwealth, which they hoped would aid in reforming the rest of the world by being "a city set on a hill" based on the true Reformed religion. Thus they were not inconsistent with their own values when they—who had been persecuted—in turn persecuted dissenters or heretics in their midst, such as the Baptist Roger Williams. He was forced to leave Massachusetts and became a founder of Rhode Island, which was set up to tolerate various "denominations" of Christians.

While the Holy Commonwealth idea was not so strongly held outside New England, there was generally in the middle and southern colonies the related concept that the various civil governments were to be in some sense a sort of Christian republic or polity, as a study of their charters will indicate. Indeed, by 1776, nine of the thirteen original colonies had an "established church" (generally Congregational in New England, Anglican in New York, Virginia, South Carolina, "Protestant" in North Carolina, with religious freedom in Rhode Island, Maryland, Pennsylvania, New Jersey, Delaware, and Georgia). After the American Revolution and adoption of state constitutions (at varying dates) most of the states disestablished the prevailing denomination, while Massachusetts and Connecticut maintained their congregational establishment for almost a third of the nineteenth century. While this did not necessarily mean that a majority of the inhabitants of these colonies were necessarily committed Christian believers, it does indicate the lingering influence of the Calvinist concept of a Christian-based civil polity as an example to a world in need of reform.

Other currents of thought, both religious and secular, swept into the colonies in the late seventeenth and early eighteenth centuries, which influenced the breakup of the Holy Commonwealth vision. Yet ironically, it was a religious movement, rather than a secular one, that did the most to break down the Puritan emphasis on a Christian state. This was the Great Awakening of the late 1730s and early 1740s (known in Britain as "the Evangelical Revival"). Wesley and Whitefield who ministered both in England and in the American colonies (as well as in Scotland), Jonathan Edwards in Massachusetts, the Tenant brothers in the middle colonies, Samuel Davies in Virginia, and many other preacher-evangelists—Congregational, Anglican, Presbyterian, and Lutheran—brought a new effectiveness, a contagious quality in preaching, that reached and transformed tens of thousands of colonists. They ascribed this new power to an outpouring of the Spirit of God.

It is difficult for us who do not live in a religiously oriented society to imagine the excitement created up and down the entire East Coast by this movement. Jonathan Edwards wrote in the *Memoirs* concerning this revival:

> This was the only subject of conversation in every company; and almost the only business of the people appeared to be, to secure their salvation. So extensive was the influence of the Spirit of God, that there was scarcely an individual in the town, either old or young, who was left unconcerned about the great things of the eternal world. . . . "The town," says Mr. Edwards, "was never so full of love, nor so full of joy, nor yet so full of distress, as it was then."[26]

On the constructive side, this powerful movement tended to break down denominational jealousies and rivalries among the Protestants and tempered them to work together in the cause of independence some three decades later. In addition to positive influence on the moral character of many persons, it seems to have been a factor in beginning to weld together the distant and disparate colonists as one people (in that the revivalists constantly and easily crossed both denominational and colonial boundary lines). Yet to the adherents of the older Holy Commonwealth vision, this movement had negative consequences as well. With its emphasis on searching one's heart for signs of personal regeneration, it unwittingly tended often to neglect commitment to the established parish system with accompanying civil responsibilities. The revival not only tended to weaken the Calvinist emphasis on closely interacting with the civil polity, but also tended to divide the churches themselves. As Bridenbaugh states: "That Congregationalists divided sharply into New Lights who favored and Old Lights who condemned the orgy of emotional enthusiasm is a twice-told tale. Churches also split over the issues of the revival. . . ."[27] Trinterud chronicles a similar 1741 division among middle colony Presbyterians, known as "New Side" (prorevival) and "Old Side" (antirevival).[28] The Old Side was more closely tied to the traditional parish-church concept, with the assumption that if one regularly attends over the years, "the means of grace" will do their work in saving the elect. The New Side wished for "new measures" such as stronger evangelistic preaching, personal confrontation over individual conversion, special meetings, etc., with frequent deemphasis on the established parish. Yet these two factions were still closely tied to the same Calvinist theology and they reunited in 1758.

In spite of this reunion, there tended to be an increasing disattachment from the civil and social aspects of "covenant." The church both in New England and in the lower colonies, pursued the Great Awakening stress on the salvation of the individual soul and purity of the church. Both of these concepts had always been part and parcel of Calvinist Christianity, but after the 1740s this emphasis among many of the population and their leadership began to outweigh church concerns for a covenantal, biblical order in civil society. This change of emphasis would take many years to reach its culmination in an eventual separation of theology from the framing of American civil government.

Other more openly secular currents of thought hastened on this process. Some competent historians of colonial America, such as

Singer, Noll, and Hatch, have emphasized a role of seventeenth-century natural law theories and the eighteenth-century secular Enlightenment on the shaping of American views of civil authority and responsibility in the pre-Revolutionary period.[29] Others, such as Bridenbaugh, have argued that the Enlightenment influence has been overstressed.[30] Though I am not prepared to assess the details of this debate, I would suggest that while the Enlightenment was important in colonial America, the more important foundational influence was from the traditional streams of Christianity (whether Calvinist in New England and the Carolina back country; Roman Catholicism in Maryland; or the Baptist and dissenter tradition in Rhode Island, Pennsylvania, Virginia, and elsewhere). It is indisputable at least that a combination of both religious and other philosophical factors combined to prepare the colonies for:

The American Revolution and Constitutional Settlement

Ironically, the same "Glorious Revolutionary Settlement" of 1688 that eventually provided American revolutionists with the British forerunner of the Bill of Rights also wrought changes in the balance between king and Parliament that proved detrimental to the earlier colonial compact tradition, and thus in a sense hastened the War of Independence. The problem for the American colonies was not unlike that of the Scottish Presbyterians after the Revolutionary Settlement and Claim of Right of 1688/89 and the Union of Parliaments in 1707. As we saw in chapter 3, the Scots (and later, the American colonials) held to a "two-powers" theory of church and state as two divinely ordained bodies, neither one deriving its power from the other, but both from God, so that neither one was subservient.

But the English Revolutionary Settlement, while clearly limiting (and thus separating civil powers),[31] still assumed a "one-power" theory, by which all power flowed from God through the people to Parliament, thus giving it a final authority over the church. In Scotland, this one-power theory was demonstrated in the 1711/12 Act of Patronage, which resulted in the 1843 Disruption of the Church of Scotland. In the colonies, the new expression (as of 1688) of the one-power theory brought problems in a different direction. The problem here was more with parliamentary interference with old colonial charters and colonial constitutional assemblies, than with the church.

According to the 1688/89 settlement, all power flowed from the Parliament. We have seen the ramifications that it had in Scotland in chapter 3. The ramifications of this theory in the American colonies were that whereas the various colonies had originally been envisioned as (at least in theory) being directly related to the king through royal charters, which allowed them liberty to form their own governmental structures, after 1688 Parliament became directly involved, even calling into question the viability of the king's charters and the colonial civil self-government authorized by the charters. These became more than theoretical matters when Parliament actually began interfering with colonial governmental and economic structures in the mid-eighteenth century through such measures as the Townshend Acts. (They were three parliamentary measures of 1767 that taxed lead, paint, glass, tea, etc.; declared that all duties on colonial goods were to be collected by British commissioners; and attempted to force colonials to trade tea with Britain only.) The departure by Parliament in the 1750s from the understanding assumed in many of the early colonial charters over a hundred years earlier played a part in feeding the flames of American revolutionary sentiment.

In the colonial constitutional tradition the colonies seem to have considered themselves a series of modified republics, covenantally bound to the king of England. A note in Bridenbaugh suggests that some colonists envisioned the relationship with the crown as something like that of the Channel Isles, which were never an official part of England, nor directly under Parliament.[32] Whether this was a generally held view in the colonies in the 1760s and 1770s (as Charles McIlwain suggests)[33] or merely a convenient argument to escape unpopular parliamentary trade restrictions, taxation, and licensing of various sorts in the colonies is debatable. Yet it is clear that the post-1688 British stress on the one authority of "the crown in Parliament" (i.e., a strictly limited constitutional monarchy in which power is almost totally exercised by Parliament) was different from the earlier colonial charter and constitutional conception, and led to increasing tensions in economic affairs once Parliament began exercising tighter control over the "king's colonies" than previously.

The events leading up to the American War of Independence and the resulting American victory and final constitutional union have been often reported. Our concern is briefly to survey key religious, political, and legal questions in the founding era, in order to assess the influence of the later Puritan tradition in American law and polity.

Not unconnected with the colonists' fear of losing the divinely ordained "rights as free Englishmen," upheld in their largely Calvinist-inspired civil compacts, was an almost perennial fear of the imposition of an Anglican episcopate over the colonies.

A serious reduction of both religious and civil liberties, as well as a disestablishment of non-Anglican churches in several of the colonies, would follow from such an application of the British "one-power theory." Bridenbaugh charts this controversy, fueled in part by the activities of the Society for the Promotion of the Gospel and frequently referred to by men such as John Adams and Ezra Stiles, who had great influence on public opinion.[34] In fact, this imposition of an episcopate never occurred, but the fear of it was a powerful ingredient in political unrest among colonists who traditionally held to a two-powers theory of church and state, rather than the one-power theory of Parliament.

Even a number of leading colonial Anglicans were so opposed to the organization of an American episcopate under "the crown in Parliament" that they threatened to become dissenters should it occur.[35] Here, as in far away Scotland, Calvinist (and Catholic) belief in two powers, civil and religious—both under God rather than one under the other—had potent political ramifications. It is not that the concern of the colonists over this matter was entirely religious; economic factors and natural law concepts of popular sovereignty and human rights, as well as Enlightenment ideas of social contract, were mixed with the older Calvinist church-state concerns.

A "Presbyterian Rebellion"

The gibe of some in the British Parliament that the American revolution was "a Presbyterian Rebellion" did not miss the mark.[36] We may include in "Presbyterian" other Calvinists such as New England

Congregationalists, many of the Baptists, and others. The long-standing New England tradition of "election day sermons" continued to play a major part in shaping public opinion toward rebellion against England on grounds of transcendent law.[37] Presbyterian preaching by Samuel Davies and others had a similar effect in preparing the climate of religious public opinion for resistance to royal or parliamentary tyranny in the name of divine law, expressed in legal covenants.[38] Davies directly inspired Patrick Henry, a young Anglican, whose Presbyterian mother frequently took him to hear Davies.[39]

Thomas C. Johnson shows that the American Presbyterians in their 1729 "Adopting Act" (adopting the Westminster Standards as their official confession of faith), had specifically denied state control over religion.[40] The Calvinists exercised continuing influence over the prerevolutionary viewpoint, not only through sermons, congregational charters, and Presbyterian "Adopting Acts," but also through higher education, as that given by President Ezra Stiles (and later Timothy Dwight) of Yale and John Witherspoon of Princeton. Witherspoon, a Scottish clergyman and supposed descendant of John Knox, who immigrated to Princeton some years before the war, taught numerous leading colonial Americans, including one president (James Madison), a vice-president, ten cabinet officers, twenty-one senators, thirty-nine congressmen and, twelve governors. He himself was the only clergyman who signed the Declaration of Independence.

Mark Noll has pointed out that from all available evidence, Witherspoon's class teaching relied heavily on Scottish Enlightenment precursors of common sense realism such as Francis Hutcheson.[41] Yet there is no doubt that he held and imparted a Calvinist view of man's fallen nature, which needs restraint by limitation and balance of powers. He taught as well a two-powers theory of church and state and a respect for divine law that gives citizens the right to resist civil tyranny.

We may think of the Declaration of Independence as having as part of its intellectual background the insistence of John Knox, Witherspoon's ancestor, on the moral duty to resist tyranny and also the French Huguenot *Vindiciae Contra Tyrannos*, a justification of rebellion on the basis of rights of the people to bring a ruler into line with the law under which his reign is bound. According to John

Adams, *Vindiciae* was one of the most important volumes circulating in prerevolutionary America.

A careful reading of the second part of the Declaration of Independence indicates its covenantal argumentation, asserting that King George III had violated the laws by which he was bound to the colonies in covenant agreement: "He has combined with others to subject us to a jurisdiction foreign to our constitution and unacknowledged by our laws, giving his assent to their pretended acts of legislation." He was then declared to be "a tyrant . . . unfit to be the ruler of a free people." As Baldwin has stated, the argument was simple: the king was alleged to be the rebel against English constitutional law, not the colonists.[42] William Henry Drayton of South Carolina drew a parallel between the illegal actions of James II (VII of Scotland) in 1688 and those of George III in 1776. If the Convention Parliament (of 1688) had the right to declare the throne vacant because of James's violations of office, so did the Continental Congress. Both kings had violated the covenant.[43]

Again, this is not to imply that the major reason why the colonists were prepared to risk rebellion was their view of the king's violation of their covenant rights. Normal desire for increased economic freedom, prosperity, greater self-determination, and other "secular" factors made them ready for war. But despite the complexity of motivation, it is significant that the legal justification for the rebellion was largely couched in covenant terminology. This in turn harked back to the previous two centuries of Calvinist experience in North America.

The influence of Calvinist religious and political theory is more difficult to trace after the successful American Revolution. Unquestionably the American Bill of Rights drew from the earlier Virginia Bill of Rights (adopted in June of 1776), of which the last clause in particular was influenced by Witherspoon's student Madison (who also wrote much of the U.S. Constitution). Madison made a successful motion to remove the idea of mere toleration of religion, which had been present in the first draft written by George Mason and Patrick Henry.

> That religion, or the duty we owe our Creator, and the manner of discharging it, can be directed only by reason and conviction, not by

> force or violence, and therefore all men are equally entitled to the free exercise of religion according to the dictates of conscience, and that it is the mutual duty of all to practice Christian forbearance, love and charity toward each other.

As Thomas C. Johnson comments, the word "toleration" (stricken at Madison's insistence from the final draft) "implied a power in the civil government to interfere with religion." Madison's statement of the rights of conscience was "very like that of the Independents in the Westminster Assembly."[44] The later First Amendment to the Constitution of the United States (1788), which required that "Congress shall make no law respecting an establishment of religion or prohibiting the free exercise thereof," was in the line of Madison and the Westminster Independents. Indeed, it was in the direct lineage of the Scottish Presbyterian conviction that state and church are two different powers, directly ordained by God, without either power originating or controlling the other.

If the Virginia Bill of Rights and the First Amendment to the U.S. Constitution both reflect aspects of the Calvinist Presbyterian two-powers doctrine, by what they do not say as well as by what they do say, yet they also (particularly the First Amendment) go in a different direction from traditional Presbyterian Calvinist church-state theory. The First Amendment, by prohibiting an established national church, certainly reflected the concerns of Baptists and others in the widespread dissenter tradition. But by this time, the Calvinists themselves were beginning to change in the direction of the dissenter tradition and away from the established state church. Presbyterians in Virginia and Carolina united with Congregationalists in New England, Baptists in Rhode Island, and Catholics in Maryland to insist that no one denomination of Christians be nationally established. The dismantling of state establishments of religion would be delayed, in some cases for three or four more decades (and so of course the First Amendment was not intended to prohibit them). As Robert Cord has argued, the First Amendment was intended to accomplish three purposes:

> First, it was intended to prevent the establishment of a national church or religion, or the giving of any religious sect or denomina-

tion a preferred status. Second, it was designed to safeguard the right of freedom of conscience in religious beliefs against invasion by the national Government. Third, it was so constructed in order to allow the States, unimpeded, to deal with religious establishments and to aid religious institutions as they saw fit. There appears to be no historical evidence that the First Amendment was intended to preclude Federal governmental aid to religion when it was provided on a nondiscriminatory basis. Nor does there appear to be any historical evidence that the First Amendment was intended to provide an absolute separation or independence of religion and the national state. The actions of the early Congresses and Presidents, in fact, suggest quite the opposite.[45]

A view very different from Cord's is presented by Thomas J. Curry.[46] Yet even if as Curry suggests, that we are to see the First Amendment as an Enlightenment fear of religious interference with the state, which Cord does not allow, it remains unarguable that underlying Calvinist themes permeate the founding documents. We see the two-powers theory of church and state and the covenantal-conciliar thesis of limitation of governmental powers in terms of divine law. Moreover, throughout the carefully ordered separation of powers with checks and balances, deliberately restraining a more unified operation of government, we see a reflection of the Calvinist doctrine of the fallenness of human nature, with its inevitable tendency of any ascendant arm of government to abuse power in a tyrannical direction. James Smylie, in a discussion of *The Federalist* number Ten and number Fifty-One, has pointed out this relationship between the Calvinist distrust of human nature and the American attempt to limit civil powers.[47]

Perhaps above all, the conviction of an enduring and divinely authored right of the people to resistance of civil or religious tyranny, while appearing in both Catholic and Lutheran tradition (as well as in the Hebraic tradition of the Old Testament), was crystallized for Americans in the previous two centuries of Puritan, Calvinist struggles. From this perspective, Calvinism bore some of its richest fruit in Scotland and later in the American republic, nurtured with a vital sap from Geneva, Huguenot France, and Puritan England.

Notes

[1] Chard Powers Smith, *Yankees and God* (New York: Hermitage House, 1954).

[2] John H. Leith, *Introduction to the Reformed Tradition* (Edinburgh: The Saint Andrew Press, 1978), p. 45.

[3] E.g., Perry Miller, *The New England Mind: The Seventeenth Century* (Cambridge, Mass.: Harvard University Press, 1954) and Miller and Johnson, *The Puritans* (Boston: American Book Company, 1938).

[4] Earnest T. Thompson, *Presbyterians in the South*, 3 vols. (Richmond, Va.: John Knox Press, 1963), 1:42, 43.

[5] Ibid., p. 43.

[6] Leonard J. Trinterud, *The Forming of an American Tradition* (Freeport: Books for Libraries Press, 1950).

[7] Donald S. Lutz, "The Origins of American Constitutionalism: The Colonial Heritage" in *Juris: For Jurisprudence and Legal History* 2 (1987): 5.

[8] Ibid., p. 8.

[9] Ibid., p. 9.

[10] Ibid., p. 10.

[11] Ibid., p. 14.

[12] Trinterud, *Forming of an American Tradition*.

[13] Lutz, "Origins of American Constitutionalism," p. 15.

[14] Ibid., p. 11.

[15] Alexis de Tocqueville, *Democracy in America* (New York: Century, 1898), 1:48.

[16] Ibid., p. 51.

[17] Lutz, "Origins of American Constitutionalism." p. 21.

[18] These changes are discussed in ibid., pp. 21-25.

[19] Ibid., p. 21.

[20] Carl Bridenbaugh, *Mitre and Sceptre: Transatlantic Faiths, Ideas, Personalities and Politics: 1689-1775* (New York: Oxford University Press, 1962), e.g., see pp. 50, 51, 215, 245, 246, 250, 251.

[21] Ibid., pp. 245, 246.

[22] Christopher Hill, *God's Englishman* (New York: Harper and Row, 1972), pp. 222, 223.

[23] Ibid., p. 238.

[24] Michael Walzer, *The Revolution of the Saints: A Study in the Origin of Radical Politics* (Cambridge, Mass.: Harvard University Press, 1965), pp. 10, 11.

[25] R. J. Rushdoony, *This Independent Republic* (Nutley, N.J.: Craig Press, 1973), p. 92.

[26] Jonathan Edwards, *Memoirs* in *The Works of Jonathan Edwards*, 2 vols. (Edinburgh: Banner of Truth, 1834, 1974), 1:xliii.

[27] Bridenbaugh, *Mitre and Sceptre*, p. 84.

[28] Trinterud, *Forming of an American Tradition*, passim.

[29] See C. Gregg Singer, A *Theological Interpretation of American History*, 2nd ed. (Phillipsburg, N.J.: Presbyterian and Reformed, 1981) and Mark A. Noll, Nathan O. Hatch, and George M. Marsden, *The Search for Christian America* (Westchester, Ill: Crossway, 1983).

[30] See Carl and Jessica Bridenbaugh, *Rebels and Gentlemen, Philadelphia in the Age of Franklin* (New York: Reynal and Hitchcock, 1942), and, e.g., Herb Titus, *Religious Freedom: The War Between Two Faiths* (Virginia Beach, Va.: CBN University, 1983).

[31] See chap. 4 of this work.

[32] Bridenbaugh, *Mitre and Sceptre*, pp. 164, 165 n. 44.

[33] Charles Howard McIlwaine, *The American Revolution: A Constitutional Interpretation* (Ithaca, N.Y.: Great Seals Books, 1958).

[34] See Bridenbaugh, *Mitre and Sceptre*, pp. 91, 97, 110, 321, 322, and Trinterud, *Forming of an American Tradition*, pp. 220, 221.

[35] Bridenbaugh, *Mitre and Sceptre*, p. 322.

[36] See the issue of *The Journal of American Church History* devoted to "Presbyterians and the American Revolution" (1976).

[37] E.g., Bridenbaugh, *Mitre and Sceptre*, pp. 190, 314.

[38] On Samuel Davies, see ibid., pp. 131, 132.

[39] See Thomas Cary Johnson, *Virginia Presbyterianism and Religious Liberty in Colonial and Revolutionary Times* (Richmond, Va.: The Presbyterian Committee of Publication, 1907), pp. 45, 46, and also Pilcher, *Samuel Davies: Apostle of Dissent in Colonial Virginia* (Knoxville: University of Tennessee Press, 1971), p. 83.

[40] Johnson, *Virginia Presbyterianism*, p. 27.

[41] Mark Noll, "James Madison: From Evangelical Princeton to the Constitutional Convention," *Pro Rege* 16, no. 2 (1987): 2-14.

[42] Alice M. Baldwin, *The New England Clergy and the American Revolution* (New York: Ungar, 1958).

[43] See Rushdoony, *This Independent Repubic*, pp. 25, 26.

[44] Johnson, *Virginia Presbyterianism*, p. 77.

[45] Robert L. Cord, *Separation of Church and State: Historical Fact and Current Fiction* (New York: Lambeth Press, 1982), p. 15.

[46] Thomas J. Curry, *The First Freedoms: Church and State in America to the Passage of the First Amendment* (Oxford: Oxford University Press, 1986).

[47] James Smylie, "Madison and Witherspoon: The Roots of American Political Theory," *Princeton University Library Chronicle* 22 (Spring 1961): 121, 126, 131.

Conclusion

JOHN CALVIN saw theology as a *scientia practica*, and so from beginning to end he integrally related doctrinal concerns with legal and political questions. He was lastingly influenced by the ancient Constantinian settlement and by late-medieval Roman Catholic conciliarism, as well as by a close study of Old Testament Hebrew polity and Roman civil law. He believed in a relatively independent church supported and reinforced by a Christian civil magistrate. In other words, Calvin held the ancient "two-powers" view that both church and state are directly ordained by God with neither subordinate to the other and neither entitled to control the other. Both have coordinate authority under God's ultimate authority, which is expressed through his infallible Word. Calvin held a much more positive view of the guidance of God's law for Christian life and polity than did Martin Luther, the elder statesman of the Reformation.

While Calvin emphasized a positive value of law, his strongly theocentric vision clearly limited the power of all human authorities and institutions of the law. They are all equally under the higher authority of God's transcendent law, including natural law engraved on the consciences of all men, and most importantly, the revealed law of Scripture. This meant that, under extreme circumstances, the people have a right to resist civil tyranny in the name of that higher covenant law, insofar as they are led by duly constituted "lesser magistrates."

The French Huguenot tractarians who followed Calvin, with their need to placate moderate Catholics in France, took Calvin's thought on the covenant basis of civil government much further in the direction of a constitutionalist view of the state by developing the concepts of natural liberty and popular sovereignty. In many respects they were ahead of their time in seeing the chief end of civil government as the protection of the liberty and safety of the people. They developed a more political (and less theological) theory of revolution on the basis of a legal, bilateral contract between ruler and people, while retaining the understanding of accountability to God for fidelity in contracts.

In Scotland, John Knox was like Calvin in holding to an essentially medieval and Catholic concept of a Christian civil magistrate protecting and reinforcing a largely independent church. But he differed from Calvin in holding to a more radical view of civil resistance. Knox, unlike Calvin, actually taught the right and duty of the common people to undertake revolution against the ruling authorities, even without the leadership of lesser magistrates if the secular authorities refused to stamp out idolatry and establish the Reformed religion. Knox developed more thoroughly than Calvin the appeal to scriptural precedents, especially of the Old Testament Hebrew theocracy, as a basis for shaping—and overturning—contemporary legal institutions.

Knox's successor, Andrew Melville, in his development of a Presbyterian ecclesiastical system at the time of growing absolutist monarchical designs on the part of James VI (I of England) emphasized the headship of Jesus Christ over his church. This carried implications for the balance of power between church and state and for the resultant liberty of the people to take whatever political action may be necessary to maintain the rights "of Christ's crown and covenant." Years of costly struggle in Scotland and England resulted in a vast increase of personal civil and ecclesiastical liberties, especially after The Glorious Revolution of 1688, not only for Scotland and England, but for much of the Western world.

The Puritan struggle during the various phases of the seventeenth-century English Revolution saw an unprecedented debate and experiments in applying in practice Calvinist-inspired covenantally based, constitutional theory. During the Commonwealth phase of the revolution, it first appeared that the Presbyterian (and Catholic) view of two independent and coordinate powers of church and state (with strong limits of state authority over individual religious and civil liberties) would prevail. But this was not to be.

The 1660 restoration of King Charles II restored also the older English one-power theory of the state. (The power of the church is held to flow through the power of the state, and in certain respects to be subordinated to it). While the final phase of the English Revolution clearly limited the power of the monarchy in 1688, it left intact the one power of "the crown in Parliament" over all things, including the church. This led to problems both in Scotland and in the American colonies, problems from which we have never fully escaped.

The American colonies were heavily influenced by large numbers of Calvinist immigrants, of both Congregational and Presbyterian persuasion. New England Congregationalists and middle and southern colony Presbyterians were united in their desire to limit the tyrannical propensities of fallen human nature by asserting covenant limits on governmental power. God reigns and his law gives his people the right to governments "instituted among men which derive their just powers from the consent of the governed." This implies the right to resist civil tyranny in terms of transcendentally based, covenant obligations binding on both ruler and ruled.

As this approach was worked out in the North American colonial and then revolutionary events, a system was developed in several states and the nation that provided historically unprecedented civil and religious liberties. This American system drew from many sources, including secular Enlightenment thought, but the Calvinist outworking of the two-powers view of church and state was prominent in the process. This view, to the Presbyterian mind, upheld the headship of Jesus Christ directly over his church without civil intermediaries. The two-powers view contributed much to the American establishment of consent of the governed, covenant or constitutional limitations of all civil power and all institutions, being seen in terms of God's transcendent law, checks and balances of power in the political and legal structure, liberty of conscience, and the inalienable right to resist tyranny, no matter how powerful or legal its pretensions.

By the late eighteenth century, Calvinism had exercised pervasive influence on civil polities throughout much of the Western world. One could argue that the practical implications of Calvinist views of personal liberties and societal structures came to play a major part in modern governmental arrangements because its theological assumptions about God's transcendent law, man's fallenness, and God's redemptive purposes for humanity were in general accord with a healthy functioning of society or even with ultimate reality. This view however would take one beyond the line of reporting the events of legal and ecclesiastical history, into the realm of interpretation by faith—a valid area of discussion, but somewhat beyond our present scope.

Yet many who would raise serious questions about aspects of Calvinist theology would accept such ideas as that the Calvinist view of man's original dignity, his present fallenness, and his possibility of redemption helped lead to a salutary development of civil means both of limiting man's tyrannical propensities and of protecting his dignity and liberty. And yet, if the influence of important Calvinist ideas (such as limitation and balance of powers) on seventeenth- and eighteenth-century civil polities represented a benevolent application of the Christian religion, it also raised a serious problem.

By the latter part of the eighteenth century there was a growing tendency for many of the major practical implications of Calvinism for civil government to enter the political "market place" disconnected from the theology that shaped them. Perhaps this was a strength in that it made these ideas and practices more widely available in a more secularized form as it combined with other strands of thought and changed its emphasis from a religious or "sectarian" to a political or "constitutional" tone. Of course, earlier Calvinist theoreticians such as Buchanan, Althusius, and the Huguenot tractarians had already taken some steps in this direction, and it could be argued that there were elements of it in Calvin's own view of natural law and the law of nations.

Yet this secularizing process also ran the danger of letting these faith-based concepts either become an end in themselves, thus losing their balanced perspective in the broader theological context and tending to idolatry, or else "run to seed" or "dry up," losing their vitality and power when long cut off from their roots in biblical faith.

Calvinist scholars in the nineteenth century, especially the Dutch, would address these concerns in the aftermath of the widespread secularization of thought and culture following the French Revolution.

Index of Persons

Index of Subjects

Douglas F. Kelly is professor of theology at Reformed Theological Seminary in Charlotte, North Carolina. He holds a B.A. degree from the University of North Carolina, an M.Div. from Union Theological Seminary, and a Ph.D. from Edinburgh University.

Dr. Kelly is a scholar marked by profound piety. His grasp of theology and his proficiency in several languages are well demonstrated in his writing, series editing, and translating. He has taught throughout the world and has served on the Jurisprudence Project of The Christian Legal Society.

CPSIA information can be obtained
at www.ICGtesting.com
Printed in the USA
FFOW01n1903150414
4866FF

9 780875 522975